BACKYARD

ENTERTAINING

GREAT TIPS FOR GRILLING

Illustrated by
DEBBIE MUMM

Publications International, Ltd.

Favorite Brand Name Recipes at www.fbnr.com

Microwave Cooking: Microwave ovens vary in wattage. Use the cooking times as guidelines and check for doneness before adding more time.

Preparation/Cooking Times: Preparation times are based on the approximate amount of time required to assemble the recipe before cooking, baking, chilling or serving. These times include preparation steps such as measuring, chopping and mixing. The fact that some preparations and cooking can be done simultaneously is taken into account. Preparation of optional ingredients and serving suggestions is not included.

Table of Contents

Grilling Basics

Grilling is a wonderful cooking technique for outstanding backyard entertaining. To get the best results, it is important that it is done correctly and safely. The following pages will explain grilling safety, charcoal grilling, different grilling methods and provide helpful information about sauces and marinades. You will also find pages and pages filled with the greatest recipes around that will make your backyard entertaining so simple and, of course, delicious.

Grilling Safety Tips

- Always position the grill on a heatproof surface away from trees and shrubbery. Make sure the grill vents are not clogged with ashes prior to starting a fire.

- To avoid flare-ups and charred foods when grilling, trim meat of excess fat.

- Keep a water-filled spray bottle near the grill to quench flare-ups.

- The best method to accurately determine doneness of large cuts of meat is to use a meat thermometer.

- Never use alcohol, gasoline or kerosene as a lighter fluid starter—all three can cause an explosion.

- To get a sluggish fire going, place two or three additional coals in a small metal can and add lighter fluid. Then, stack them on the coals in the grill and light with a match.

4

• Remember that hot coals create a very hot grill, grid, tools and food. Always wear oven mitts to protect your hands.

• The number of coals required for barbecuing depends on the size and type of grill and the amount of food to be prepared. As a general rule, it takes about 30 coals to grill one pound of meat.

• Always serve cooked meats and poultry on a clean platter, not the one that held the raw food.

Checking Charcoal Temperature

Whether you're cooking vegetables or steaks on the grill, use the temperature called for in the recipe. A quick, easy way to estimate the temperature of the coals is to hold your hand, palm side down, about 4 inches above the coals. Count the number of seconds you can hold your hand in that position before the heat forces you to pull it away.

Seconds	Coal Temperature
2	Hot, 375°F or more
3	Medium-hot, 350°F or 375°F
4	Medium, 300°F to 350°F
5	Low, 200°F to 300°F

Grilling Methods

Direct Cooking Method

The food is placed on the grid directly over the coals. Make sure there is enough charcoal in a single layer to extend 1 or 2 inches beyond the area of food. This method is for quick-cooking steaks, chops, hamburgers, kabobs and seafood.

Indirect Cooking Method

The food is placed on the grid over a metal or disposable foil drip pan, with the coals banked either to one side or on both sides of the pan. This method is for slow, even cooking of foods such as large cuts of meat and whole chickens. When grilling by indirect cooking for more than 45 minutes, extra briquets will need to be added to maintain a constant temperature.

Foil Wrap Method

Foods, either plain or with fresh herbs, a sauce or a small amount of liquid, can also be wrapped in foil and placed on the grill. This will help the food cook faster and keep it moist.

Charcoal Grilling Information

- To light a charcoal fire, arrange the coals in a pyramid shape 20 to 30 minutes prior to cooking. The pyramid shape provides enough ventilation for the coals to catch. To start with lighter fluid, soak the coals with about $1/2$ cup of lighter fluid. Wait one minute to allow the fluid to soak into the coals, then light with a match.

- To light a charcoal fire using a chimney starter, remove the grid from the grill and place the chimney starter in the base of the grill. Crumple a few sheets of newspaper and place them in the bottom portion of the chimney starter. Fill the top portion with coals. Light the newspaper. The coals should be ready in about 20 to 30 minutes.

- The coals are ready when they are about 80% ash-gray during daylight and glowing at night.

To lower the cooking temperature, spread the coals farther apart or raise the grid farther away from coals. To raise the cooking temperature, either lower the grid or move the coals closer together and tap off the ash.

Making Marinades and Sauces

- Marinades enhance the flavor of food and those with an acidic ingredient help tenderize tougher cuts of meat.

- Heavy-duty resealable plastic bags are ideal to hold foods as they marinate. Turn marinating foods occasionally to let the flavor penetrate evenly.

- Marinate foods in the refrigerator, not at room temperature.

- Never baste foods during the last 5 minutes of grilling with a marinade that was used to marinate meat, poultry or a seafood item. Marinades can be used as basting and dipping sauces after the food is removed by boiling them for a minimum of 1 minute. This will kill any harmful bacteria that may have contaminated the marinades.

- Basting sauces containing sugar, honey or tomato products should be applied near the end of the grilling process. This will prevent the food from charring.

- Basting sauces made from seasoned oils and butters may be brushed on throughout grilling. Oils and butter prevent leaner cuts of meat from drying out.

Black Bean Mexicali Salad

1 can (15 ounces) black beans, rinsed and drained
1 cup fresh or thawed frozen corn
6 ounces roasted red bell peppers, cut in thin strips
   or coarsely chopped
½ cup chopped red or yellow onion, divided
⅓ cup mild chipotle or regular salsa
2 tablespoons cider vinegar
2 ounces mozzarella cheese, cut in ¼-inch cubes

Place all ingredients except 1 tablespoon of the onion and
the cheese in medium mixing bowl. Toss gently to blend
well. Let stand 15 minutes to absorb flavors. Just before
serving, gently fold in all but 2 tablespoons of cheese.
Sprinkle remaining cheese and onion on top.

Makes 7 servings

Note: Serve within 30 minutes to take advantage of flavors at
their peak.

8

Black Bean Mexicali Salad

Three-Bean Salad

1 (15½-ounce) can red kidney beans
1 (14½-ounce) can cut green beans
1 (14½-ounce) can yellow wax beans
1 green bell pepper, seeded and chopped
1 medium onion, chopped
2 ribs celery, sliced
¾ cup cider vinegar
⅓ cup FILIPPO BERIO® Olive Oil
2 tablespoons sugar
   Salt and freshly ground black pepper

Rinse and drain kidney beans; drain green and wax beans. In large bowl, combine beans, bell pepper, onion and celery. In small bowl, whisk together vinegar, olive oil and sugar. Pour over bean mixture; toss until lightly coated. Cover; refrigerate several hours or overnight before serving. Season to taste with salt and black pepper. Store salad, covered, in refrigerator up to 1 week.

Makes 10 to 12 servings

BBQ Ranch Chicken Salad

Prep Time: 15 minutes
Cook Time: 10 minutes

- ½ cup KRAFT® Original Barbecue Sauce
- 1 pound boneless skinless chicken breasts, cut into strips
- 1 package (10 ounces) mixed salad greens
- 1 large tomato, cut into wedges
- ½ cup sliced red onion
- ½ cup KRAFT LIGHT DONE RIGHT® Ranch Reduced Fat Dressing
- ¼ cup crumbled blue cheese

HEAT barbecue sauce in skillet on medium-high heat. Add chicken; cook and stir until chicken is cooked through. Add additional barbecue sauce, if desired.

TOSS greens, tomato and onion in large bowl. Top with chicken. Pour dressing over greens mixture. Sprinkle with cheese.

Makes 6 servings

Variation: Place boneless skinless chicken breast halves on greased grill over medium coals. Grill 12 to 15 minutes or until cooked through, turning and brushing frequently with barbecue sauce. Slice chicken; serve over greens mixture.

Marinated Tomatoes & Mozzarella

1 cup chopped fresh basil leaves
1 pound Italian tomatoes, sliced
½ pound fresh packed buffalo mozzarella cheese, sliced
¼ cup olive oil
3 tablespoons chopped fresh chives
2 tablespoons red wine vinegar
2 teaspoons sugar
½ teaspoon dried oregano
½ teaspoon LAWRY'S® Seasoned Pepper
½ teaspoon LAWRY'S® Garlic Powder with Parsley
   Fresh basil leaves (optional)

In large resealable plastic food storage bag, combine all ingredients except whole basil leaves; mix well. Marinate in refrigerator at least 30 minutes. To serve, arrange tomato and cheese slices on serving plate. Garnish with whole basil leaves, if desired.   *Makes 4 to 6 servings*

Serving Suggestion: Serve with grilled chicken sandwiches or as a zesty Italian appetizer.

Wholesome Tip

Buffalo mozzarella is the most prized of all fresh mozzarellas. It is made from a combination of buffalo milk and cow's milk. Other types of fresh mozzarella may be substituted for the buffalo mozzarella.

Smoked Turkey & Pepper Pasta Salad

Prep Time: 15 minutes plus refrigerating

   ¾ cup **MIRACLE WHIP® Salad Dressing**
   1 tablespoon **GREY POUPON® Dijon Mustard**
   ½ teaspoon **dried thyme leaves**
   8 ounces **fettucini, cooked, drained**
   1 cup **cubed LOUIS RICH® Oven Roasted Turkey Breast**
   ¾ cup **zucchini slices, cut into halves**
   ½ cup **red bell pepper strips**
   ½ cup **yellow bell pepper strips**
      Salt and black pepper

• MIX salad dressing, mustard and thyme until well blended.

• ADD pasta, turkey and vegetables; mix lightly. Season with salt and pepper to taste. Refrigerate until chilled.

• ADD additional dressing before serving, if desired.

Makes about 5 to 6 servings

Cool and Creamy Pea Salad
with Cucumbers and Red Onion

  2 tablespoons finely chopped red onion
  1 tablespoon reduced-fat mayonnaise
  ⅛ teaspoon salt
  ⅛ teaspoon black pepper
  ½ cup frozen green peas, thawed
  ¼ cup diced red bell pepper
  ¼ cup diced cucumber

1. Combine onion, mayonnaise, salt and black pepper in medium bowl; stir until well blended.

2. Add remaining ingredients and toss gently to coat.

Makes 2 (½-cup) servings

Wholesome Tip

This creamy salad will make a great side dish to any hamburger meal.

Summertime Vegetable Salad

2 tablespoons butter or margarine
3 cups canned diced tomatoes, drained
2 cups zucchini, sliced and halved
2 cups fresh or thawed frozen corn
⅓ cup chopped onion
¼ teaspoon black pepper

Melt butter in large nonstick skillet over medium-high heat. Add tomatoes, zucchini, corn, onion and pepper. Cook 5 minutes or until vegetables are tender, stirring occasionally. Serve warm or cover and refrigerate until ready to serve.   *Makes 6 servings*

Wholesome Tip

Choose zucchini that are heavy for their size, firm and well shaped. They should have a bright color and be free of cuts and any soft spots. Small zucchini are more tender because they are harvested when they are young.

Tuna and Bean Salad

 1 can (8 ounces) broad or lima beans
 1 can (15 ounces) cannellini beans (white kidney beans)
 ½ red onion, thinly sliced
 2 cans (6 ounces each) tuna in oil, undrained
 ⅓ cup olive or vegetable oil
 2 tablespoons red wine vinegar
   Black pepper
 ½ cup pitted ripe olives
 2 tablespoons chopped fresh parsley
   Flat-leaf parsley
   Italian or French bread, if desired

Rinse beans under cold running water and drain thoroughly.
Combine beans and onion in large bowl. Add tuna, breaking into
large flakes with fork. Blend oil, vinegar and pepper in small
bowl; pour over tuna mixture. Add olives and chopped parsley;
toss to mix well. Spoon onto individual serving plates; garnish
with flat-leaf parsley. Serve with crusty Italian or French bread,
if desired.   *Makes 6 servings*

Tag-Along Fruit Salad

Citrus Dressing
    ¼ **cup CRISCO® Oil***
    ¼ **cup orange juice**
    2 **tablespoons lemon juice**
    2 **tablespoons sugar**
    ¼ **teaspoon paprika**

Salad
    1 **can (20 ounces) pineapple chunks in juice, drained**
    2 **cups seedless green grapes**
 1¼ **cups miniature marshmallows****
    1 **cup fresh orange sections**
    1 **cup sliced fresh pears*****
    1 **cup sliced banana*****
    1 **cup sliced apples*****
    ½ **cup maraschino cherries, halved**

Use your favorite Crisco Oil product.

**1 cup raisins may be substituted for marshmallows.*

***Add Citrus Dressing to sliced apples, pears and bananas immediately after slicing to prevent discoloration.*

1. *For dressing,* combine oil, orange juice, lemon juice, sugar and paprika in container with tight-fitting lid. Shake well.

2. Combine pineapple, grapes, marshmallows, oranges, pears, banana, apples and cherries in large bowl. Shake dressing. Pour over salad. Toss to coat. Cover. Refrigerate. Garnish, if desired.

Makes 10 servings

Red Bean & Corn Salad with Lime-Cumin Dressing

  2 tablespoons fresh lime juice
1½ teaspoons canola oil
  ½ teaspoon ground cumin
  ½ teaspoon water
  ⅛ teaspoon salt
  ¾ cup canned red beans, rinsed and drained
  ½ cup frozen corn with bell pepper and onion, thawed
  ¼ cup chopped tomato
  2 tablespoons chopped green onion, divided
  2 large romaine lettuce leaves

1. Whisk together lime juice, oil, cumin, water and salt in medium bowl.

2. Add beans, corn, tomato and 1 tablespoon green onion; toss to coat. Serve on lettuce leaves. Top with remaining green onion.

Makes 1 serving

Wholesome Tip

Double the ingredients in this recipe to make two servings of this delicious salad.

Orange Orzo Salad

8 ounces BARILLA® Orzo
4 tablespoons olive oil
4 tablespoons orange juice
3 tablespoons grated orange peel
   Salt and pepper
2 oranges, peeled, cut into sections and chopped
1 cup golden raisins
⅓ cup chopped green onions
2 tablespoons chopped cilantro

1. Cook orzo according to package directions; drain.

2. To prepare orange vinaigrette, combine olive oil, orange juice and orange peel; mix well. Add salt and pepper to taste.

3. Combine orzo, oranges, raisins, green onions and cilantro in serving bowl. Add orange vinaigrette; toss to coat. Chill before serving.

Makes 6 to 8 servings

Coal-Roasted Potato Salad

Lemon Dijon Dressing (recipe follows)
1½ pounds small red or white potatoes, cut into 1-inch chunks
Olive oil
1½ teaspoons dried thyme leaves
Salt and black pepper
2 medium yellow onions, cut into ½-inch-thick slices

Prepare Lemon Dijon Dressing. Toss potatoes with 1 tablespoon oil, thyme, salt and pepper. Insert wooden picks into onion slices from edges to prevent separating into rings. (Soak wooden picks in hot water 15 minutes to prevent burning.) Brush lightly with oil. Grill potatoes and onions on covered grill over medium KINGSFORD® Briquets about 30 minutes until golden brown and tender, turning occasionally. Remove picks from onions; separate into rings. Place potatoes and onions in large bowl; toss with dressing. Serve warm. *Makes 4 servings*

Lemon Dijon Dressing: Whisk together 3 tablespoons olive oil, 1 tablespoon white wine vinegar, 1 tablespoon *each* chopped green onion and parsley, 1½ teaspoons lemon juice and ½ teaspoon Dijon mustard. Season to taste with salt and pepper.

Stuffed Portobello Mushrooms

Prep Time: none
Cook Time: 30 minutes

- **1 box UNCLE BEN'S® Long Grain & Wild Rice Roasted Garlic**
- **2 tablespoons prepared pesto sauce**
- **8 ounces cream cheese, softened**
- **4 large portobello mushrooms**
  Salt and black pepper to taste
- **1 large tomato**
- **4 tablespoons grated Parmesan cheese**
- **4 basil leaves (optional)**

COOK: Preheat oven to 400°F. CLEAN: Wash hands. Prepare rice according to package directions. Meanwhile, stir pesto into cream cheese until well blended. Remove stems from mushrooms. Clean mushroom caps well. Place mushrooms, stem side up, on baking sheet. Sprinkle with salt and pepper. Spread one fourth of cream cheese mixture onto each mushroom. Top with ½ cup cooked rice. Slice tomato into 4 thick slices. Place 1 slice on top of rice and sprinkle each mushroom with 1 tablespoon Parmesan cheese. Bake 10 minutes.

SERVE: Serve each mushroom on a separate plate and garnish with basil leaf, if desired.

CHILL: Refrigerate leftovers immediately.   *Makes 4 servings*

Sassy Corn on the Cob

1 cup (2 sticks) unsalted butter or margarine, softened
2 teaspoons TABASCO® brand Pepper Sauce
8 ears unhusked fresh corn

Preheat grill. Combine butter and TABASCO® Sauce in small bowl; mix well. Peel one side of corn husk away from cob without removing completely, and loosen remaining husk. Do not remove silk. Brush butter mixture over kernels and smooth back husk to original shape.

Place corn on oiled grid over medium heat and grill 15 to 20 minutes, turning every 5 minutes. (Outside husk will be charred.)   *Makes 8 servings*

Grilled Vegetables with Olive Sauce

Prep and Cook Time: 20 minutes

2 frozen thawed ears sweet corn, cut into rounds
2 large yellow pattypan squash, coarsely chopped
1 medium zucchini, thinly sliced
   Vegetable oil
¼ cup butter, melted
6 green olives with pimientos, finely chopped
1 tablespoon lemon juice
¼ teaspoon dried parsley flakes
1 container (16 ounces) cottage cheese

1. Prepare grill for direct cooking. Place corn, squash and zucchini on prepared vegetable grilling grid; brush with oil and season with salt and pepper to taste.

2. Grill vegetables, on covered grill, over hot coals 10 minutes or until crisp-tender, turning halfway. Remove; keep warm.

3. Combine butter, olives, lemon juice and parsley; stir well.

4. Place vegetables on serving platter; drizzle with 2 tablespoons olive sauce. Serve with cottage cheese and remaining olive sauce.

Makes 4 servings

Vegetable Couscous

Prep Time: 5 minutes
Cook Time: 10 minutes

3 cups water
1 package KNORR® Recipe Classics™ Vegetable Soup,
   Dip and Recipe Mix
2 tablespoons BERTOLLI® Olive Oil or I CAN'T
   BELIEVE IT'S NOT BUTTER!® Spread
1 package (10 ounces) plain couscous (about 1½ cups)
¼ cup chopped fresh parsley (optional)
   Pine nuts, slivered almonds or raisins (optional)

• In 2-quart saucepan, bring water, recipe mix and olive oil to a boil, stirring frequently. Reduce heat; cover and simmer 2 minutes.

• Stir couscous into saucepan until evenly moistened. Remove from heat; cover and let stand 5 minutes.

• Fluff couscous with fork. Spoon into serving dish. Garnish, if desired, with chopped parsley and nuts or raisins.

Makes 5 cups couscous

Recipe Tip: Turn Vegetable Couscous into an easy one-dish meal. Just add 2 cups cut-up cooked chicken or turkey to the saucepan in step 1.

Velveeta® Twice Baked Ranch Potatoes

Prep Time: 20 minutes plus baking potatoes
Bake Time: 20 minutes

  4 baking potatoes
  ½ cup KRAFT® Ranch Dressing
  ¼ cup BREAKSTONE'S® or KNUDSEN® Sour Cream
  1 tablespoon OSCAR MAYER® Real Bacon Bits
  ¼ pound (4 ounces) VELVEETA® Pasteurized Prepared
      Cheese Product, cut up

1. Bake potatoes at 400°F for 1 hour. Slice off tops of potatoes; scoop out centers, leaving ⅛-inch shell.

2. Mash potato centers. Add dressing, sour cream and bacon bits; beat until fluffy. Stir VELVEETA into potato mixture. Spoon into shells.

3. Bake at 350°F for 20 minutes.   *Makes 4 servings*

How to Bake Potatoes: Russet potatoes are best for baking. Scrub potatoes well, blot dry and rub the skin with a little oil and salt. Prick the skin of the potatoes with a fork so steam can escape. Stand them on end in a muffin tin. Bake at 400°F for 1 hour or until tender.

Salads & Sides - 25

Vegetable Potato Salad

Prep Time: 20 minutes
Chill Time: 2 hours

**1 envelope LIPTON® RECIPE SECRETS® Vegetable Soup
    Mix**
1 cup HELLMANN'S® or BEST FOODS® Mayonnaise
2 teaspoons white vinegar
**2 pounds red or all-purpose potatoes, cooked and cut
    into chunks**
¼ cup finely chopped red onion (optional)

1. In large bowl, combine soup mix, mayonnaise and vinegar.

2. Add potatoes and onion; toss well. Chill 2 hours.

Makes 6 servings

Cob Corn in Barbecue Butter

    4 ears fresh corn, shucked
    2 tablespoons butter or margarine, softened
    ½ teaspoon dry barbecue seasoning
    ¼ teaspoon salt
       Cherry tomato wedges and Italian parsley for garnish

1. Pour 1 inch of water into large saucepan or skillet. (Do not add salt, as it will make corn tough.) Bring to a boil over medium-high heat. Add ears; cover. Cook 4 to 7 minutes until kernels are slightly crisp when pierced with fork.*

2. Remove corn with tongs to warm serving platter. Blend butter, barbecue seasoning and salt in small bowl until smooth. Serve immediately with corn. Garnish, if desired.   *Makes 4 servings*

Length of cooking time depends on size and age of corn.

Wholesome Tip

To shuck corn, pull outer husks down the ear to the base. Snap off the husks and stem at the base. Strip away the silk from the corn by hand. Remove any remaining silk with a dry vegetable brush or a corn-silk brush. Trim any blemishes from the corn and rinse under cold running water.

Sweet & Tangy Marinated Vegetables

8 cups mixed fresh vegetables, such as broccoli,
cauliflower, zucchini, carrots and red bell peppers,
cut into 1 to 1½-inch pieces
⅓ cup distilled white vinegar
¼ cup sugar
¼ cup water
1 packet (1 ounce) HIDDEN VALLEY® The Original
Ranch® Salad Dressing & Seasoning Mix

Place vegetables in a gallon size Glad® Zipper Storage Bag. Whisk together vinegar, sugar, water and salad dressing & seasoning mix until sugar dissolves; pour over vegetables. Seal bag and shake to coat. Refrigerate 4 hours or overnight, turning bag occasionally.

Makes 8 servings

Note: Vegetables will keep up to 3 days in refrigerator.

Sherried Mushrooms

½ cup butter
1 cup HOLLAND HOUSE® Sherry Cooking Wine
1 garlic clove, crushed
18 fresh mushrooms, sliced
Salt and black pepper

Melt butter in medium skillet over medium heat. Add cooking wine and garlic. Add mushrooms; cook until tender, about 5 minutes, stirring frequently. Season to taste with salt and pepper.

Makes 2 to 3 servings

Wholesome Tip

When buying mushrooms, look for those that are firm and evenly colored with tightly closed caps. Avoid ones that are slimy or have any soft dark spots.

Sweet Potato Salad

Prep Time: 15 minutes
Total Time: 45 minutes

**1½ pounds sweet potatoes or yams, scrubbed, quartered
   lengthwise and cut crosswise into ¾-inch pieces
   (2 large or 3 medium potatoes)**
3 tablespoons cider vinegar
2 tablespoons sweet pickle relish
2 teaspoons Dijon mustard
½ teaspoon salt
¼ teaspoon freshly ground black pepper
½ cup CRISCO® Oil*
2 scallions or green onions, trimmed and thinly sliced
¼ cup finely chopped red bell pepper (optional)

Use your favorite Crisco Oil product.

1. Place potato slices in vegetable steamer.** Place steamer over 2-inches of water in large pot. Cover pot. Bring to a boil on high heat. Steam potatoes 10 to 15 minutes, or until tender when pierced with knife. Remove steamer from pan. Peel potatoes when cool enough to handle (about 10 minutes). Place potatoes in mixing bowl.

2. Combine vinegar, pickle relish, mustard, salt and black pepper in jar with tight-fitting lid. Shake well. Add oil. Shake well again.

3. Toss warm potatoes with dressing. Add scallions and red pepper, if used. Serve at room temperature or chilled.

Makes 4 servings

***Boil for 10 to 15 minutes if steamer is not available.*

Note: This salad can be made up to one day in advance and refrigerated, tightly covered with plastic wrap.

Grilled Vegetables al Fresco

2 large red bell peppers
2 medium zucchini
1 large eggplant

Spicy Marinade
⅔ cup white wine vinegar
½ cup soy sauce
2 tablespoons minced ginger
2 tablespoons olive oil
2 tablespoons sesame oil
2 large cloves garlic, minced
2 teaspoons TABASCO® brand Pepper Sauce

Seed red peppers; cut each pepper into quarters. Cut each zucchini lengthwise into ¼-inch thick strips. Slice eggplant into ¼-inch-thick rounds.

In 13×9-inch baking dish, combine Spicy Marinade ingredients. Place vegetable pieces in mixture; toss to mix well. Cover and refrigerate vegetables at least 2 hours or up to 24 hours, turning occasionally.

About 30 minutes before serving, preheat grill to medium heat, placing rack 5 to 6 inches above coals. Place red peppers, zucchini and eggplant slices on grill rack. Grill vegetables 4 minutes, turning once and brushing with marinade occasionally.

Makes 4 servings

To Broil: Preheat oven broiler and broil vegetables 5 to 6 inches below broiler flame for 4 minutes on each side.

Easy Cole Slaw

Prep Time: 10 minutes
Total Time: 30 minutes

2 tablespoons CRISCO® Oil*
¼ cup granulated sugar
¼ cup cider vinegar
1 tablespoon prepared mustard
½ teaspoon salt
¼ teaspoon freshly ground black pepper
1 bag (1 pound) cole slaw mix (or shredded cabbage)

Use your favorite Crisco Oil product.

1. Combine oil, sugar, vinegar, mustard, salt and pepper in small saucepan. Place pan on medium heat. Simmer for 3 minutes.

2. Place cole slaw mix in mixing bowl. Toss with hot dressing. Let stand for 20 minutes. Serve with slotted spoon.

Makes 4 servings

Note: This cole slaw can also be made up to 2 days in advance and refrigerated, tightly covered. Drain before serving.

Herbed Corn on the Cob

1 tablespoon butter or margarine
1 teaspoon mixed dried herb leaves, such as basil,
oregano, sage and rosemary
⅛ teaspoon salt
Black pepper
4 ears corn, husks removed

Microwave Directions

1. Combine butter, herbs, salt and pepper in small microwavable bowl. Microwave at MEDIUM (50%) 30 to 45 seconds or until butter is melted.

2. With pastry brush, coat corn with butter mixture. Place corn on microwavable plate; microwave at HIGH 5 to 6 minutes. Turn corn over and microwave at HIGH 5 to 6 minutes until tender.

Makes 4 servings

Ranch Picnic Potato Salad

**6 medium potatoes (about 3½ pounds), cooked, peeled
    and sliced**
½ cup chopped celery
¼ cup sliced green onions
2 tablespoons chopped parsley
1 teaspoon salt
⅛ teaspoon black pepper
1 cup HIDDEN VALLEY® The Original Ranch® Dressing
1 tablespoon Dijon mustard
2 hard-cooked eggs, finely chopped
    Paprika
    Lettuce (optional)

Combine potatoes, celery, onions, parsley, salt and pepper in a
large bowl. Stir together dressing and mustard in a small bowl;
pour over potato mixture and toss lightly. Cover and refrigerate
several hours. Sprinkle with eggs and paprika. Serve in a lettuce-
lined bowl, if desired.   *Makes 8 servings*

Wholesome Tip

To hard cook eggs, place the eggs in a
single layer in a saucepan. Add cold
water to cover the eggs by one inch.
Cover and bring to a boil over high
heat. Remove from the heat. Let stand
15 minutes. Immediately pour off the
water, cover with cold water or ice
water and let stand until cooled.

Grilled Asparagus

1 pound fresh asparagus
CRISCO® No-Stick Cooking Spray
½ teaspoon salt
¼ teaspoon freshly ground black pepper

1. Prepare charcoal or gas grill. Trim woody stems off asparagus by breaking stalks. Spray asparagus with Crisco No-Stick Cooking Spray.

2. Grill asparagus for 3 minutes. Turn spears with tongs. Grill 3 to 4 minutes. Sprinkle with salt and pepper. Serve immediately.

Makes 4 servings

Green Beans with Toasted Pecans

    3 tablespoons I CAN'T BELIEVE IT'S NOT BUTTER!®
      Spread, melted
    1 teaspoon sugar
    ¼ teaspoon garlic powder
      Pinch ground red pepper
      Salt to taste
    ⅓ cup chopped pecans
    1 pound green beans

In small bowl, blend I Can't Believe It's Not Butter! Spread, sugar, garlic powder, pepper and salt.

In 12-inch nonstick skillet, heat 2 teaspoons garlic mixture over medium-high heat and cook pecans, stirring frequently, 2 minutes or until pecans are golden. Remove pecans and set aside.

In same skillet, heat remaining garlic mixture and stir in green beans. Cook, covered, over medium heat, stirring occasionally, 6 minutes or until green beans are tender. Stir in pecans.

Makes 4 servings

Wholesome Tip

This recipe will work best with very fresh slender young beans.

Southwestern Potato Salad

5 large red or white boiling potatoes (about 2 pounds total)
   Boiling water
¼ pound bacon
½ cup canned diced green chilies, drained
⅓ cup chopped fresh parsley
¼ cup finely chopped onion
⅓ cup vegetable oil
3 tablespoons white wine vinegar
½ teaspoon salt
¼ teaspoon black pepper
¼ teaspoon ground cumin
3 drops hot pepper sauce

Place potatoes in large saucepan with 2 inches of boiling water. Cook, covered, 20 to 25 minutes or until tender. Drain and let stand until cool. Meanwhile, place bacon in large skillet; cook over medium-high heat until crisp. Drain bacon on paper towels. Let cool slightly; crumble. Cut potatoes into cubes; place in large bowl. Add bacon, chilies, parsley and onion; mix lightly. Whisk remaining ingredients in small bowl until well blended. Pour over potato mixture; toss gently to coat potatoes evenly. Cover and refrigerate 2 hours for flavors to blend.   *Makes 6 to 8 servings*

Steaks, Chops & More

Grilled Sherry Pork Chops

¼ cup HOLLAND HOUSE® Sherry Cooking Wine
¼ cup GRANDMA'S® Molasses
2 tablespoons soy sauce
4 pork chops (1 inch thick)

In plastic bowl, combine sherry, molasses and soy sauce; pour over pork chops. Cover; refrigerate 30 minutes. Prepare grill. Drain pork chops; reserve marinade. Grill pork chops over medium-high heat 20 to 30 minutes or until pork is no longer pink in center, turning once and brushing frequently with reserved marinade. Discard any remaining marinade.*

Makes 4 servings

Do not baste during last 5 minutes of grilling.

Grilled Sherry Pork Chops and
Grilled Asparagus (page 35)

Southwestern Kabobs

4 boneless top loin pork chops, cut into 1-inch cubes
4 tablespoons taco or fajita seasoning
½ green bell pepper, seeded and cut into 1-inch pieces
½ large onion peeled, cut into 1-inch pieces

In a plastic bag or shallow bowl, toss together pork cubes with desired seasoning until pork is evenly coated. Thread pork cubes, alternating with pepper and onion pieces, onto skewers.* Grill over a medium-hot fire, turning occasionally, until pork is nicely browned.   *Makes 4 servings*

If using wooden skewers, soak in water for 20 minutes before using.

Favorite recipe from **National Pork Board**

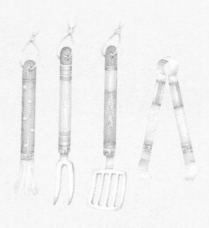

Spicy Grilled Pork Chops

¼ **cup minced onion**
¼ **cup soy sauce**
2 **tablespoons fresh lime juice**
2 **cloves garlic, minced**
½ **teaspoon red pepper flakes**
4 **center cut well-trimmed pork loin or rib chops, cut**
   ¾ **inch thick**

1. Combine onion, soy sauce, lime juice, garlic and crushed red pepper in large resealable plastic food storage bag; add chops. Close bag securely; turn to coat. Marinate in refrigerator at least 4 hours or up to 24 hours, turning once.

2. Drain chops; reserve marinade. Brush with some of the reserved marinade. Grill or broil chops, 5 to 6 inches from heat, 7 minutes. Turn chops over; brush with marinade, discarding remaining marinade. Grill or broil 8 to 13 minutes until barely pink in center.   *Makes 4 servings*

Wholesome Tip

Marinades add unique flavor to foods and help tenderize less-tender cuts of meat. Turn marinating foods occasionally to let the flavor infuse evenly.

Steak Provençal

4 sirloin, tenderloin or ribeye steaks (about 11 ounces each)

5 tablespoons I CAN'T BELIEVE IT'S NOT BUTTER!® Spread

2 large cloves garlic, finely chopped

1½ cups chopped tomatoes (about 2 medium)

1 to 2 tablespoons rinsed and chopped large capers

¼ teaspoon salt

¼ teaspoon ground black pepper

2 tablespoons chopped fresh parsley

Grill or broil steaks to desired doneness.

Meanwhile, in 10-inch skillet, melt I Can't Believe It's Not Butter! Spread and cook garlic over medium heat, stirring occasionally, 30 seconds. Add tomatoes, capers, salt and pepper. Cook, stirring occasionally, 3 minutes or until tomatoes are cooked and mixture is saucy. Stir in parsley. Serve over hot steaks.

Makes 4 servings

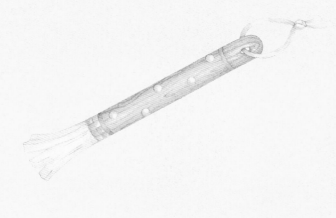

Roscoe's Ribs

1 to 2 tablespoons LAWRY'S® Seasoned Salt
5 pounds beef or pork ribs
1 cup Worcestershire sauce
¾ cup apple cider vinegar
1 tablespoon olive oil
½ teaspoon minced garlic

Sprinkle Seasoned Salt over ribs. In large resealable plastic food storage bag, combine Worcestershire, vinegar, oil and garlic; mix well. Remove at least ½ cup marinade for basting. Add ribs; seal bag. Marinate in refrigerator at least 1 hour. Remove ribs; discard used marinade. Grill over low heat or bake ribs in 350°F. oven 1 to 1¼ hours or until no longer pink, turning and basting often with additional ½ cup marinade. *Makes 4 to 6 servings*

Hint: For extra flavor, marinate ribs overnight.

Wholesome Tip

Serve these flavorful ribs with coleslaw and baked beans for a classic barbecue meal.

Grilled Meat Loaf

1½ pounds ground chuck or ground sirloin
½ cup seasoned dry bread crumbs
⅔ cup chili sauce, divided
⅓ cup grated onion
1 egg
½ teaspoon black pepper
¼ teaspoon salt
2 tablespoons packed light brown sugar
1 tablespoon spicy brown or Dijon mustard

Prepare barbecue grill for direct cooking. Combine beef, bread crumbs, ⅓ cup chili sauce, onion, egg, pepper and salt in large bowl; mix well. On cutting board or cookie sheet, shape mixture into 9×5-inch oval loaf, 1½ inches thick.

Combine remaining ⅓ cup chili sauce, sugar and mustard in small bowl; mix well. Set aside. Place meat loaf on grid. Grill meat loaf, on covered grill, over medium-hot coals 10 minutes. Carefully turn meat loaf over using 2 large spatulas.

Brush chili sauce mixture over top of meat loaf. Continue to grill, covered, 10 to 12 minutes until no longer pink in center. (If desired, insert instant-read thermometer* into center of thickest part of meat loaf. Thermometer should register 160°F.) Let stand 10 minutes before slicing. Serve with mashed potatoes and peas and carrots, if desired. *Makes 4 to 6 servings*

*Do not leave instant-read thermometer in meat loaf during grilling since thermometer is not heatproof.

Grilled Chili-Marinated Pork

3 tablespoons ground seeded dried pasilla chilies
1 teaspoon coarse or kosher salt
½ teaspoon ground cumin
2 tablespoons vegetable oil
1 tablespoon fresh lime juice
3 cloves garlic, minced
2 pounds pork tenderloin or thick boneless pork loin chops, trimmed of fat
Shredded romaine lettuce (optional)
Radishes for garnish

1. Mix chilies, salt and cumin in small bowl. Stir in oil and lime juice to make smooth paste. Stir in garlic.

2. Butterfly pork by cutting lengthwise about ⅔ of the way through, leaving meat in one piece; spread meat flat. Cut tenderloin crosswise into 8 equal pieces. Do not cut chops into pieces.

3. Place pork between pieces of plastic wrap. Pound with flat side of meat mallet to ¼-inch thickness.

4. Spread chili paste on both sides of pork pieces to coat evenly. Place in shallow glass baking dish. Marinate, covered, in refrigerator 2 to 3 hours.

5. Prepare coals for grill or preheat broiler. Grill or broil pork 6 inches from heat 8 to 10 minutes for grilling or 6 to 7 minutes for broiling, turning once. Serve on lettuce-lined plate. Garnish, if desired. *Makes 6 to 8 servings*

Margarita Pork Kabobs

1 cup margarita drink mix *or* 1 cup lime juice,
    4 teaspoons sugar and ½ teaspoon salt
1 teaspoon ground coriander
1 clove garlic, minced
1 pound pork tenderloin, cut into 1-inch cubes
2 tablespoons margarine, melted
2 teaspoons lime juice
1 tablespoon minced fresh parsley
⅛ teaspoon sugar
1 large green or red bell pepper, cut into 1-inch cubes
2 ears corn, cut into 8 pieces

For marinade, combine margarita mix, coriander and garlic in
small bowl. Place pork cubes in large resealable plastic food
storage bag; pour marinade over pork. Close bag securely; turn to
coat. Marinate for at least 30 minutes. Combine margarine, lime
juice, parsley and sugar in small bowl; set aside. Thread pork
cubes onto four skewers, alternating with pieces of bell pepper
and corn. (If using bamboo skewers, soak in water 20 to
30 minutes before using to prevent them from burning.) Grill over
hot coals for 15 to 20 minutes or until barely pink in center,
basting with margarine mixture and turning frequently.

Makes 4 servings

Favorite recipe from **National Pork Board**

America's Favorite Pork Chops

4 top loin pork chops
¾ cup Italian dressing
1 teaspoon Worcestershire sauce

Place all ingredients in a self-sealing bag; seal bag and place in refrigerator for at least 20 minutes (or as long as overnight). Remove chops from bag, discarding marinade. Grill over medium-hot fire, turning once, until just done, about 8 to 15 minutes total cooking time (depending upon thickness of chops).

Makes 4 servings

Favorite recipe from **National Pork Board**

Wholesome Tip

Serve this American favorite with another, such as coleslaw or potato salad.

Grilled Beef with Two Sauces

1 (1-pound) boneless beef sirloin steak

Roasted Garlic Sauce
- **¾ cup mayonnaise**
- **¼ cup Roasted Garlic Purée (recipe follows)**
- **¼ cup GREY POUPON® Dijon Mustard**
- **1 tablespoon lemon juice**
- **2 tablespoons chopped parsley**

Sundried Tomato Sauce
- **¾ cup chopped roasted red peppers**
- **½ cup sundried tomatoes, chopped**
- **3 tablespoons GREY POUPON® Dijon Mustard**
- **2 tablespoons chopped parsley**
- **2 to 3 tablespoons olive oil**
- **¼ teaspoon crushed red pepper flakes**

1. Grill beef over medium heat to desired doneness and refrigerate.

2. For Roasted Garlic Sauce, blend all ingredients in medium bowl. Refrigerate at least 1 hour to blend flavors.

3. For Sundried Tomato Sauce, combine roasted red peppers, sundried tomatoes, mustard and parsley in medium bowl. Slowly add oil as needed to bind. Add red pepper flakes. Refrigerate at least 1 hour to blend flavors. Bring to room temperature before serving.

4. Slice beef and arrange on 4 serving plates. Spoon about 2 tablespoons of each sauce onto each plate. Serve with sliced tomatoes and cooled steamed asparagus; garnish as desired.

Makes 4 servings

Roasted Garlic Purée: Remove excess papery skin of 1 head garlic and separate into cloves. Place in 8×8×2-inch baking pan. Add 2 to 3 tablespoons olive oil and 1 cup chicken broth. Bake at 350°F for 25 to 30 minutes or until garlic is soft. Cool and squeeze garlic pulp from skins; discard liquid in pan.

Mustard-Glazed Ribs

¾ **cup beer**
½ **cup firmly packed dark brown sugar**
½ **cup spicy brown mustard**
 3 **tablespoons soy sauce**
 1 **tablespoon ketchup**
¾ **teaspoon TABASCO® brand Pepper Sauce**
½ **teaspoon ground cloves**
 4 **pounds pork spareribs or beef baby back ribs**

Combine beer, sugar, mustard, soy sauce, ketchup, TABASCO®
Sauce and cloves in medium bowl; mix well. Position grill rack as
far from coals as possible. Place ribs on grill over low heat. For
pork ribs, grill 45 minutes; turn occasionally. Brush with mustard
glaze. Grill 30 minutes longer or until meat is cooked through;
turn and baste ribs often with mustard glaze. (For beef baby back
ribs, grill 15 minutes. Brush with mustard glaze. Grill 30 minutes
longer or until meat is cooked to desired doneness; turn and baste
ribs often with mustard glaze.) Heat any remaining glaze to a
boil; serve with ribs.   *Makes 4 servings*

Honey Mustard
Steaks with Grilled Onions

Prep Time: 30 minutes

- **4 boneless beef top loin steaks, cut 1 inch thick**
- **⅓ cup coarse-grain Dijon-style mustard**
- **1 tablespoon chopped parsley**
- **1 tablespoon plus 1½ teaspoons honey**
- **1 tablespoon cider vinegar**
- **1 tablespoon water**
- **¼ teaspoon hot pepper sauce**
- **⅛ teaspoon coarse grind black pepper**
- **1 large red onion, sliced ½ inch thick**

Combine mustard, parsley, honey, vinegar, water, hot pepper sauce and pepper. Place beef steaks and onion on grid over medium coals; brush both with mustard mixture. Grill 9 to 12 minutes for rare (140°F) to medium (160°F), turning once and brushing with mustard mixture. *Makes 4 servings*

Favorite recipe from **North Dakota Beef Commission**

Tijuana Blackened Steak

¾ **teaspoon garlic powder**
¾ **teaspoon onion powder**
¾ **teaspoon ground black pepper**
½ **teaspoon ground white pepper**
¼ **teaspoon ground red pepper**
 4 **(4- to 6-ounce) beef shell or strip steaks, about ½ inch
    thick**
½ **cup A.1.® Steak Sauce**
¼ **cup margarine or butter, melted**

1. Mix garlic powder, onion powder and peppers; spread on waxed paper. Coat both sides of steaks with seasoning mixture.

2. Blend steak sauce and margarine. Grill steaks 10 to 15 minutes or until done, turning and brushing often with ¼ cup steak sauce mixture. Serve steaks with remaining steak sauce mixture.

Makes 4 servings

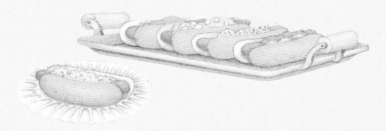

Cowboy Kabobs

½ cup A.1.® Original or A.1.® BOLD & SPICY Steak
    Sauce
½ cup barbecue sauce
2½ teaspoons prepared horseradish
1 (1½-pound) beef top round steak, cut into ½-inch
    strips
4 medium-size red skin potatoes, cut into wedges,
    blanched
1 medium onion, cut into wedges
⅓ cup red bell pepper strips
⅓ cup green bell pepper strips
⅓ cup yellow bell pepper strips

Soak 8 (10-inch) wooden skewers in water at least 30 minutes.

Blend steak sauce, barbecue sauce and horseradish; set aside.

Alternately thread steak strips (accordion style) and vegetables
onto skewers. Place kabobs in nonmetal dish; coat with ⅔ cup
reserved steak sauce mixture. Cover; refrigerate 1 hour, turning
occasionally.

Remove kabobs from marinade; discard marinade. Grill kabobs
over medium heat or broil 6 inches from heat source 6 to
10 minutes or until steak is desired doneness, turning occasionally
and basting with remaining steak sauce mixture. Serve
immediately. *Makes 4 servings*

Grilled Apple-Stuffed Pork Chops

Prep Time: 20 minutes
Cook Time: 40 minutes

5 tablespoons *French's*® Zesty Deli Mustard, divided
3 tablespoons honey, divided
1 cup corn bread stuffing mix
1 small McIntosh apple, peeled, cored and chopped
¼ cup minced onion
¼ cup chopped fresh parsley
4 rib pork chops, cut 1¼ inches thick (about 2 pounds)

1. Combine ¼ cup water, 2 tablespoons mustard and 1 tablespoon honey in medium bowl. Add stuffing mix, apple, onion and parsley; toss until crumbs are moistened. Combine remaining 3 tablespoons mustard and 2 tablespoons honey in small bowl; set aside for glaze.

2. Cut horizontal slits in pork chops, using sharp knife, to make pockets for stuffing. Spoon stuffing evenly into pockets. Secure openings with toothpicks.

3. Place pork chops on oiled grid. Grill over medium heat 40 to 45 minutes until no longer pink near bone, turning often. Baste chops with reserved glaze during last 10 minutes of cooking.

Makes 4 servings

Mushroom-Sauced Steak

½ **cup sliced onion**
2 **tablespoons margarine or butter**
1½ **cups sliced mushrooms**
1 **cup A.1.® BOLD & SPICY Steak Sauce**
½ **cup dairy sour cream**
2 **(8-ounce) beef club or strip steaks, about 1 inch thick**

Sauté onion in margarine in medium skillet over medium heat until tender, about 5 minutes. Add mushrooms; sauté 5 minutes more. Stir in steak sauce; heat to a boil. Reduce heat and simmer 5 minutes; stir in sour cream. Cook and stir until heated through (do not boil); keep warm.

Grill steaks over medium heat 5 minutes on each side or until done. Serve steaks topped with mushroom sauce.

Makes 4 servings

Honey-Lime Pork Chops

**1 envelope LIPTON® RECIPE SECRETS® Savory Herb
with Garlic Soup Mix***
⅓ cup soy sauce
3 tablespoons honey
3 tablespoons lime juice
1 teaspoon grated fresh ginger *or* **¼ teaspoon ground
ginger (optional)**
4 pork chops, 1½ inches thick

*Also terrific with LIPTON® RECIPE SECRETS® Garlic Mushroom or
Onion Soup Mix.*

1. For marinade, blend all ingredients except pork chops.

2. In shallow baking dish or plastic bag, pour ½ cup of the
marinade over chops; turn to coat. Cover, or close bag, and
marinate in refrigerator, turning occasionally, 2 to 24 hours.
Refrigerate remaining marinade.

3. Remove chops from marinade, discarding marinade. Grill or
broil chops, turning once and brushing with refrigerated
marinade, until chops are done.   *Makes 4 servings*

Honeyed Pork and Mango Kabobs

Prep Time: 30 minutes
Marinate Time: 1 hour
Cook Time: about 20 minutes

½ cup honey
¼ cup frozen apple juice concentrate, thawed
3 tablespoons *Frank's*® *RedHot*® Cayenne Pepper Sauce
¼ teaspoon ground allspice
1 teaspoon grated lemon peel
1 pound pork tenderloin, cut into 1-inch cubes
1 large (12 ounces) ripe mango, peeled, pitted and cut into ¾-inch cubes, divided
½ cup frozen large baby onions, partially thawed

1. Combine honey, juice concentrate, **Frank's RedHot** Sauce and allspice in small saucepan. Bring to a boil over medium heat. Reduce heat to low; cook, stirring, 5 minutes. Stir in lemon peel. Remove from heat. Pour ¼ cup marinade into small bowl; reserve.

2. Place pork in large resealable plastic food storage bag. Pour remaining marinade over pork. Seal bag; refrigerate 1 hour. Prepare grill.

3. To prepare dipping sauce, place ¼ cup mango cubes in blender or food processor. Add reserved ¼ cup marinade. Cover; process until puréed. Transfer to serving bowl; set aside.

4. Alternately thread pork, remaining mango cubes and onions onto metal skewers. Place skewers on oiled grid. Grill,* over medium-low coals, 12 to 15 minutes or until pork is no longer pink. Serve kabobs with dipping sauce.

Makes 6 servings (¾ cup sauce)

Or, broil 6 inches from heat 10 to 12 minutes or until pork is no longer pink.

Note: You may substitute 1½ cups fresh or frozen peach cubes (2 to 3 peaches) for fresh mango.

Grilled Caribbean Steaks

6 tablespoons brown sugar
2 tablespoons plus 1½ teaspoons paprika
2 tablespoons granulated sugar
1 tablespoon kosher salt
1 tablespoon chili powder
1¼ teaspoons garlic powder
1¼ teaspoons dried oregano leaves
1¼ teaspoons dried basil leaves
¾ teaspoon dried thyme leaves
¾ teaspoon celery seed
¼ teaspoon cayenne pepper
2 lean beef T-bone steaks (12 to 16 ounces each), 1 inch thick

To prepare spice mix, combine all ingredients except steak in small bowl; mix well. Measure out ¼ cup spice mix, reserving remaining for other uses.* Rub steaks with ¼ cup spice mix, using 1 tablespoon per side. Refrigerate steaks, covered, overnight or up to 3 days. Grill steaks on covered grill over medium KINGSFORD® Briquets 12 to 14 minutes for medium-rare or to desired doneness, turning once.

Makes 4 to 6 servings

Recipe for spice mix makes 1¼ cups. Store leftover spice mix in covered container in cool, dry place. Use with beef, pork or chicken.

Apricot-Mustard Grilled Pork Tenderloin

1 pork tenderloin, about 1 pound
3 tablespoons apricot preserves
5 tablespoons honey mustard

Season tenderloin with salt and pepper; in small bowl stir together the preserves and mustard. Grill pork over a medium-hot fire, brushing with mustard mixture frequently, turning once or twice, until just done, about 15 minutes.   *Makes 4 servings*

Favorite recipe from **National Pork Board**

Wholesome Tip

The best way to test for doneness of beef, pork, fish and poultry is to use a meat thermometer or an instant-read thermometer. But, you may want to try this quick beef touch test first: Gently press a piece of uncooked flesh to feel what rare feels like; the flesh will become tighter and more resistant as it cooks. Medium will have some give; well-done will be quite firm.

Grilled Honey Garlic Pork Chops

¼ **cup lemon juice**
¼ **cup honey**
2 **tablespoons soy sauce**
1 **tablespoon dry sherry**
2 **cloves garlic, minced**
4 **boneless center-cut lean pork chops (about 4 ounces each)**

Combine all ingredients except pork chops in small bowl. Place pork in shallow baking dish; pour marinade over pork. Cover and refrigerate 4 hours or overnight. Remove pork from marinade. Heat remaining marinade in small saucepan over medium heat to a simmer. Grill pork over medium-hot coals 12 to 15 minutes, turning once during cooking and basting frequently with marinade, until meat thermometer registers 155° to 160°F.

Makes 4 servings

Favorite recipe from **National Honey Board**

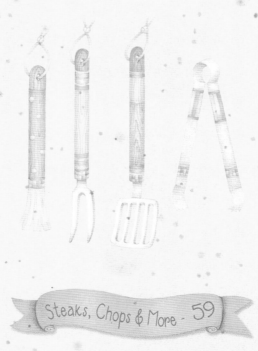

Steaks, Chops & More - 59

Jamaican Baby Back Ribs

2 tablespoons sugar
2 tablespoons fresh lemon juice
1 tablespoon salt
1 tablespoon vegetable oil
2 teaspoons black pepper
2 teaspoons dried thyme leaves, crushed
¾ teaspoon ground cinnamon
¾ teaspoon ground nutmeg
¾ teaspoon ground allspice
½ teaspoon ground red pepper
6 pounds well-trimmed pork baby back ribs, cut into
   3- to 4-rib portions
   Barbecue Sauce (recipe page 172)

1. For seasoning rub, combine all ingredients except ribs and Barbecue Sauce in small bowl; stir well. Spread over all surfaces of ribs; press with fingertips so mixture adheres to ribs. Cover; refrigerate overnight.

2. Prepare grill for indirect cooking. While coals are heating, prepare barbecue sauce.

3. Baste ribs generously with Barbecue Sauce; grill 30 minutes more or until ribs are tender and browned, turning occasionally.

4. Bring remaining Barbecue Sauce to a boil over medium-high heat; boil 1 minute. Serve ribs with remaining sauce.

Makes 6 servings

Ginger Beef and Pineapple Kabobs

**1 cup LAWRY'S® Thai Ginger Marinade with Lime Juice,
divided**
1 can (16 ounces) pineapple chunks, juice reserved
1½ pounds sirloin steak, cut into 1½-inch cubes
2 red bell peppers, cut into chunks
2 medium onions, cut into wedges

In large resealable plastic food storage bag, combine ½ cup Thai
Ginger Marinade and 1 tablespoon pineapple juice; mix well. Add
steak, bell peppers and onions; seal bag. Marinate in refrigerator
at least 30 minutes. Remove steak and vegetables; discard used
marinade. Alternately thread steak, vegetables and pineapple onto
skewers. Grill or broil skewers 10 to 15 minutes or until desired
doneness, turning once and basting often with additional ½ cup
Thai Ginger Marinade. Do not baste during last 5 minutes of
cooking. Discard any remaining marinade.   *Makes 6 servings*

Wholesome Tip

For a complete and great-tasting
meal, serve kabobs with a light salad
and bread.

Hot and Spicy Flank Steak

¼ **cup vegetable oil**
2 **tablespoons red wine vinegar**
2 **tablespoons sherry**
2 **tablespoons soy sauce**
2 **tablespoons brown sugar**
2 **teaspoons LAWRY'S® Seasoned Salt**
1½ **to 2 teaspoons red pepper flakes**
1 **teaspoon Worcestershire sauce**
1 **teaspoon paprika**
1 **teaspoon chili powder**
½ **teaspoon LAWRY'S® Garlic Powder with Parsley**
1½ **pounds flank steak, scored across grain on both sides**

In large resealable plastic food storage bag, combine all
ingredients except steak; mix well. Remove ¼ cup marinade for
basting. Add steak; seal bag. Marinate in refrigerator at least
1 hour. Remove steak from marinade; discard used marinade.
Grill or broil steak until desired doneness, about 10 to 12 minutes,
turning once and basting often with additional ¼ cup marinade.
Do not baste during last 5 minutes of cooking. Discard any remaining
marinade. Thinly slice steak on the diagonal across the grain.

Makes 4 to 6 servings

Serving Suggestion: Serve with grilled halved potatoes brushed with
oil and sprinkled with Lawry's® Garlic Salt.

Onion-Marinated Steak

2 large red onions
¾ cup plus 2 tablespoons WISH-BONE® Italian Dressing*
1 (2- to 3-pound) boneless sirloin or London broil steak

*Also terrific with Wish-Bone® Robusto Italian or Just 2 Good Italian Dressing.

Cut 1 onion in half; refrigerate one half. Chop remaining onion to equal 1½ cups. In blender or food processor, process 1 cup Italian dressing and chopped onion until puréed.

In large, shallow nonaluminum baking dish or plastic bag, pour 1¾ cups dressing-onion marinade over steak; turn to coat. Cover, or close bag, and marinate in refrigerator, turning occasionally, 3 to 24 hours. Refrigerate remaining ½ cup marinade.

Remove steak from marinade, discarding marinade. Grill or broil steak, turning and brushing frequently with refrigerated marinade, until steak is done.

Meanwhile, in saucepan, heat remaining 2 tablespoons Italian dressing and cook remaining onion half, cut into thin rings, stirring occasionally, 4 minutes or until tender. Serve over steak.

Makes 8 servings

Burgers

Ranchero Onion Burgers

Prep Time: 10 minutes
Cook Time: 10 minutes

1 pound ground beef
½ cup salsa
½ cup (2 ounces) shredded Monterey Jack cheese
1⅓ cups *French's*® French Fried Onions, divided
½ teaspoon garlic powder
¼ teaspoon ground black pepper
4 hamburger rolls

Combine beef, salsa, cheese, ⅔ *cup* French Fried Onions, garlic powder and pepper in large bowl. Shape into 4 patties.

Place patties on oiled grid. Grill* over medium coals 10 minutes or until no longer pink in center, turning once. Serve on rolls. Garnish with additional salsa, if desired. Top with remaining ⅔ *cup* onions.   *Makes 4 servings*

Or, broil 6 inches from heat.

Tip: For extra-crispy warm onion flavor, heat French Fried Onions in the microwave for 1 minute. Or, place in foil pan and heat on the grill 2 minutes.

Ranchero Onion Burger and
Ranch Picnic Potato Salad (page 34)

Garden Garlic Burgers

1½ pounds ground beef or turkey
**1 envelope LIPTON® RECIPE SECRETS® Savory Herb
with Garlic Soup Mix***
2 small carrots, finely shredded
1 small zucchini, shredded
1 egg, slightly beaten
¼ cup plain dry bread crumbs

Also terrific with LIPTON® RECIPE SECRETS® Onion, or Onion-Mushroom Soup Mix.

1. In large bowl, combine all ingredients; shape into 6 patties.

2. Grill or broil until no longer pink in center. Serve, if desired, on hamburger buns or whole wheat rolls.   *Makes 6 servings*

Wholesome Tip

Serve these tasty burgers with homemade French fries or potato salad.

Apple Turkey Burgers

 1 pound ground turkey
 1 Granny Smith apple, peeled, cored and grated
 ½ teaspoon ground coriander
 ½ teaspoon salt
 ¼ teaspoon black pepper
 1 (8-ounce) can jellied cranberry sauce
 ½ teaspoon dry mustard
 ⅛ teaspoon cinnamon
 ⅛ teaspoon nutmeg
 4 hamburger buns

1. Preheat charcoal grill for direct-heat cooking.

2. In medium bowl, combine turkey, apple, coriander, salt and pepper. Evenly divide turkey mixture into 4 burgers, approximately 3½ inches in diameter. Grill turkey burgers 5 to 6 minutes per side or until 160°F on meat thermometer and meat is no longer pink in center.

3. In small bowl, combine cranberry sauce, mustard, cinnamon and nutmeg.

4. To serve, place 1 burger on bottom half of each bun. Spoon sauce over burgers and top with other half of bun.

Makes 4 servings

Favorite recipe from **National Turkey Federation**

Blue Cheese Burgers

1¼ **pounds lean ground beef**
 1 **tablespoon finely chopped onion**
1½ **teaspoons chopped fresh thyme** *or* ½ **teaspoon dried
      thyme leaves**
 ¾ **teaspoon salt**
    Dash black pepper
 4 **ounces blue cheese, crumbled**

Preheat grill.

Combine ground beef, onion, thyme, salt and pepper in medium
bowl; mix lightly. Shape into 8 patties.

Place cheese in center of 4 patties to within ½ inch of outer edge;
top with remaining patties. Press edges together to seal.

Grill 8 minutes or until no longer pink in center (160°F), turning
once. Serve with lettuce, tomatoes and Dijon mustard on whole
wheat buns, if desired.   *Makes 4 servings*

Hawaiian-Style Burgers

1½ pounds ground beef
⅓ cup chopped green onions
2 tablespoons Worcestershire sauce
⅛ teaspoon black pepper
⅓ cup pineapple preserves
⅓ cup barbecue sauce
6 pineapple slices
6 hamburger buns, split and toasted

1. Combine beef, onions, Worcestershire and pepper in large bowl. Shape into six 1-inch-thick patties.

2. Combine preserves and barbecue sauce in small saucepan. Bring to a boil over medium heat, stirring often.

3. Place patties on grill rack directly above medium coals. Grill, uncovered, until no longer pink in center (160°F), turning and brushing often with sauce. Place pineapple on grill; grill 1 minute or until browned, turning once.

4. To serve, place patties on buns with pineapple.

Makes 6 servings

Broiling Directions: Arrange patties on rack in broiler pan. Broil 4 inches from heat until no longer pink in center (160°F), turning and brushing often with sauce. Broil pineapple 1 minute, turning once.

Easy Salmon Burgers
with Honey Barbecue Sauce

⅓ cup honey
⅓ cup ketchup
1½ teaspoons cider vinegar
1 teaspoon prepared horseradish
¼ teaspoon minced garlic
⅛ teaspoon crushed red pepper flakes (optional)
1 can (7½ ounces) salmon, drained
½ cup dried bread crumbs
¼ cup chopped onion
3 tablespoons chopped green bell pepper
1 egg white
2 hamburger buns, toasted

In small bowl, combine honey, ketchup, vinegar, horseradish, garlic and red pepper flakes until well blended. Set aside half of sauce. In separate bowl, mix together salmon, bread crumbs, onion, green pepper and egg white. Blend in 2 tablespoons remaining sauce. Divide salmon mixture into 2 patties, ½ to ¾ inch thick. Place patties on well-oiled grill, 4 to 6 inches from hot coals. Grill, turning 2 to 3 times and basting with sauce, until burgers are browned and cooked through. Or place patties on lightly greased baking sheet. Broil 4 to 6 inches from heat source, turning 2 to 3 times and basting with remaining sauce, until cooked through. Place on hamburger buns and serve with reserved sauce. *Makes 2 servings*

Favorite recipe from **National Honey Board**

Grilled Feta Burgers

½ **pound lean ground sirloin**
½ **pound ground turkey breast**
2 **teaspoons grated lemon peel**
1 **teaspoon olive oil**
1 **teaspoon dried oregano leaves**
¼ **teaspoon salt**
⅛ **teaspoon black pepper**
1 **ounce feta cheese**
  Cucumber Raita (recipe follows)
4 **slices tomato**
4 **whole wheat hamburger buns**

1. Combine sirloin, turkey, lemon peel, oil, oregano, salt and pepper; mix well and shape into 8 patties. Make small depression in each of 4 patties and place ¼ of the cheese in each depression. Cover each with remaining 4 patties, sealing edges to form burgers.

2. Grill burgers 10 to 12 minutes or until thoroughly cooked (160°F), turning once. Serve with Cucumber Raita and tomato slice on whole wheat bun.   *Makes 4 burgers*

Cucumber Raita

1 **cup plain nonfat yogurt**
½ **cup finely chopped cucumber**
1 **tablespoon minced fresh mint leaves**
1 **clove garlic, minced**
¼ **teaspoon salt**

Combine all ingredients in small bowl. Cover and refrigerate until ready to use.

California Turkey Burgers

Prep Time: 15 minutes
Cook Time: 15 minutes

   1 pound ground turkey
   ½ cup finely chopped cilantro
   ⅓ cup plain dry bread crumbs
   3 tablespoons *French's*® Classic Yellow® Mustard
   1 egg, beaten
   ½ teaspoon salt
   ¼ teaspoon black pepper
   8 thin slices (3 ounces) Monterey Jack cheese
   ½ red or yellow bell pepper, seeded and cut into rings
   4 hamburger buns

1. Combine turkey, cilantro, bread crumbs, mustard, egg, salt and pepper in large bowl. Shape into 4 patties, pressing firmly.

2. Place patties on oiled grid. Grill over high heat 15 minutes or until no longer pink in center. Top burgers with cheese during last few minutes of grilling. Grill pepper rings 2 minutes. To serve, place burgers on buns and top with pepper rings. Serve with additional mustard, if desired. *Makes 4 servings*

Cheddar-Stuffed Mesquite Burgers

½ cup LAWRY'S® Mesquite Marinade with Lime Juice
1 pound ground beef
½ cup chopped green bell pepper
½ cup finely chopped onion
¼ cup unseasoned bread crumbs
½ teaspoon LAWRY'S® Seasoned Pepper
½ cup (2 ounces) shredded cheddar cheese
4 hamburger buns, toasted
  Lettuce leaves
  Tomato slices

In large bowl, combine Mesquite Marinade, ground beef, bell pepper, onion, bread crumbs and Seasoned Pepper; mix well. Let stand 20 minutes. Shape meat into 8 thin patties. In center of 4 patties, place layer of cheese. Top with remaining patties. Press edges tightly together to seal. Grill or broil burgers 8 to 10 minutes or until no longer pink in center (160°F), turning halfway through grilling time. Serve burgers on toasted buns with lettuce and tomato.   *Makes 4 servings*

Hint: Ground turkey is an excellent substitute for ground beef.

Mexicali Burgers

Guacamole (recipe follows)
1 pound ground beef
⅓ cup prepared salsa or picante sauce
⅓ cup crushed tortilla chips
3 tablespoons finely chopped fresh cilantro
2 tablespoons finely chopped onion
1 teaspoon ground cumin
4 slices Monterey Jack or Cheddar cheese
4 kaiser rolls or hamburger buns, split
Lettuce leaves (optional)
Sliced tomatoes (optional)

To prevent sticking, spray grill with nonstick cooking spray.
Prepare coals for grilling. Meanwhile, prepare Guacamole.

Combine beef, salsa, tortilla chips, cilantro, onion and cumin in
medium bowl until well blended. Shape mixture into 4 burgers.
Place burgers on grill, 6 inches from medium coals. Grill, covered,
8 to 10 minutes for medium or until no longer pink in center
(160°F), turning once. Place 1 slice cheese on each burger during
last 1 to 2 minutes of grilling. If desired, place rolls, cut side
down, on grill to toast lightly during last 1 to 2 minutes of
grilling. Place burgers between rolls; top burgers with Guacamole.
Serve with lettuce and tomatoes. Garnish as desired.

Makes 4 servings

Guacamole

1 ripe avocado, seeded
1 tablespoon salsa or picante sauce
1 teaspoon lime or lemon juice
¼ teaspoon garlic salt

Place avocado in medium bowl; mash with fork until avocado is
slightly chunky. Add salsa, lime juice and garlic salt; blend well.

Makes about ½ cup

Fresh Rockfish Burgers

8 ounces skinless rockfish or scrod fillet
1 egg white *or* 2 tablespoons egg substitute
¼ cup dry bread crumbs
1 green onion, finely chopped
1 tablespoon finely chopped fresh parsley
2 teaspoons fresh lime juice
1½ teaspoons capers
1 teaspoon Dijon mustard
¼ teaspoon salt
⅛ teaspoon black pepper
Nonstick cooking spray
4 grilled whole wheat English muffins
4 leaf lettuce leaves
4 slices red or yellow tomato
Additional Dijon mustard for serving (optional)

1. Finely chop rockfish and place in medium bowl. Add egg white, bread crumbs, onion, parsley, lime juice, capers, mustard, salt and pepper; gently combine with fork. Shape into 4 patties.

2. Spray heavy grillproof cast iron skillet or griddle with nonstick cooking spray; place on grid over hot coals to heat. Spray tops of burgers with additional cooking spray. Place burgers in hot skillet; grill on covered grill over hot coals 4 to 5 minutes or until burgers are browned on both sides, turning once. Serve on English muffins or buns with lettuce, tomato slice and Dijon mustard, if desired. *Makes 4 servings*

Big D Ranch Burgers

1 cup sliced onions
⅓ cup green bell pepper strips
⅓ cup red bell pepper strips
1 tablespoon margarine or butter
3 tablespoons A.1.® Steak Sauce
2 teaspoons prepared horseradish
1 pound ground beef
4 onion rolls, split

Cook onions, green pepper and red pepper in margarine in skillet over medium heat until tender-crisp. Stir in steak sauce and horseradish; keep warm.

Shape ground beef into 4 burgers. Grill burgers over medium heat for 5 minutes on each side or until no longer pink in center (160°F). Place burgers on roll bottoms; top each with ¼ cup pepper mixture and roll top. Serve immediately.

Makes 4 servings

Tempting Taco Burgers

1 envelope LIPTON® RECIPE SECRETS® Onion-
   Mushroom Soup Mix*
1 pound ground beef
½ cup chopped tomato
¼ cup finely chopped green bell pepper
1 teaspoon chili powder
¼ cup water

Also terrific with LIPTON® RECIPE SECRETS® Onion, Beefy Onion or Beefy Mushroom Soup Mix.

1. In large bowl, combine all ingredients; shape into 4 patties.

2. Grill or broil until no longer pink in center (160°F). Serve, if desired, on hamburger buns and top with shredded lettuce and Cheddar cheese.   *Makes 4 servings*

Wholesome Tip

To make this a Tex-Mex meal, serve these burgers with tortilla chips and guacamole.

Italian Sausage Turkey Burgers

1 pound ground turkey
1 pound Italian turkey sausage
8 hamburger buns
8 tablespoons bottled marinara sauce
8 slices low-fat mozzarella cheese

1. Preheat charcoal grill for direct-heat cooking.

2. In large bowl combine ground turkey and Italian sausage. Shape mixture into 8 burgers approximately 3½ inches in diameter. Grill burgers 5 to 6 minutes per side or until 160°F is reached on meat thermometer and meat is no longer pink in center.

3. To serve, place burgers on bottom halves of buns. Top each burger with 1 tablespoon marinara sauce, 1 slice mozzarella cheese and other half of bun. *Makes 8 servings*

Favorite recipe from **National Turkey Federation**

Cajun Chicken Burgers

1 pound fresh ground chicken *or* turkey
1 small onion, finely chopped
¼ cup chopped bell pepper
3 scallions, minced
1 clove garlic, minced
1 teaspoon Worcestershire sauce
½ teaspoon TABASCO® brand Pepper Sauce
   Dash ground pepper

Combine all ingredients in medium bowl. Form into 4-inch patties. Broil or grill 4 to 6 minutes on each side or until cooked through (160°F). Serve immediately. *Makes 5 servings*

Scandinavian Burgers

1 pound lean ground beef
¾ cup shredded zucchini
⅓ cup shredded carrots
2 tablespoons finely minced onion
1 tablespoon fresh chopped dill *or* 1 teaspoon dried dill
    weed
½ teaspoon salt
    Dash black pepper
1 egg, beaten
¼ cup beer

Preheat grill.

Combine ground beef, zucchini, carrots, onion, dill, salt and pepper in medium bowl; mix lightly. Stir in egg and beer. Shape into four patties.

Grill 8 minutes or until no longer pink in center (160°F), turning once. Serve on whole wheat buns or rye rolls, if desired.

Makes 4 servings

Hometown Burgers

　　1 **pound ground beef**
　　¾ **cup thinly sliced mushrooms**
　　¼ **cup finely chopped onion**
　　¼ **teaspoon salt**
　　　Generous dash black pepper
　　⅓ **cup barbecue sauce**
　　4 **hamburger buns, split, toasted and buttered**
　　　Lettuce leaves
　　　Tomato slices
　　　Sliced onion

In large bowl, combine beef, mushrooms, onion, salt and pepper. Shape into four 1-inch-thick patties.

Place patties on grill rack directly above medium coals. Grill, uncovered, until no longer pink in center (160°F), turning and brushing often with barbecue sauce. Place patties on buns with lettuce, tomato and sliced onion. *Makes 4 servings*

Southwest Pesto Burgers

Make-Ahead Time: up to 3 weeks in refrigerator
Final Prep and Cook Time: 20 minutes

Cilantro Pesto
    1 large clove garlic
    4 ounces fresh cilantro, stems removed and rinsed
  1½ teaspoons bottled minced jalapeño pepper* *or*
        1 tablespoon bottled sliced jalapeño pepper,*
        drained
    ¼ teaspoon salt
    ¼ cup vegetable oil

Burgers
  1¼ pounds ground beef
    ¼ cup plus 1 tablespoon Cilantro Pesto, divided
    ½ teaspoon salt
    4 slices pepper Jack cheese
    2 tablespoons light or regular mayonnaise
    4 kaiser rolls, split
    1 ripe avocado, peeled and sliced
    Salsa

*Jalapeño peppers can sting and irritate the skin; wear rubber gloves when handling peppers and do not touch eyes. Wash hands after handling peppers.

1. For pesto, with motor running, drop garlic through feed tube of food processor; process until minced. Add cilantro, jalapeño pepper and salt; process until cilantro is chopped.

2. With motor running, slowly add oil through feed tube; process until thick paste forms. Transfer to container with tight-fitting lid. Store in refrigerator up to 3 weeks.

3. To complete recipe, prepare barbecue grill for direct cooking.

continued on page 83

4. Combine beef, ¼ cup pesto and salt in large bowl; mix well. Form into 4 patties. Place patties on grid over medium-hot coals. Grill, uncovered, 4 to 5 minutes per side or until meat is no longer pink in center (160°F). Add cheese to patties during last 1 minute of grilling.

5. While patties are cooking, combine mayonnaise and remaining 1 tablespoon pesto in small bowl; mix well. Top patties with mayonnaise mixture. Serve on rolls with avocado and salsa.

Makes 4 servings

Serving Suggestion: Serve with refried beans.

Zesty Burgers

    2 pounds ground beef
    ½ cup WISH-BONE® Italian Dressing*
    2 tablespoons horseradish (optional)
    1 carrot, grated
    1 medium onion, finely chopped
    2 eggs
    1 cup plain dry bread crumbs

Also terrific with Wish-Bone® Robusto Italian Dressing.

In large bowl, combine all ingredients; shape into 6 patties. Grill or broil until burgers are no longer pink in center (160°F). Serve, if desired, on hamburger rolls.

Makes 6 servings

Chutney Turkey Burgers

 1 pound ground turkey
½ cup purchased chutney, divided
½ teaspoon salt
½ teaspoon black pepper
⅛ teaspoon hot pepper sauce
½ cup nonfat yogurt
 1 teaspoon curry powder
 4 hamburger buns

1. Preheat charcoal grill for direct-heat cooking.

2. In medium bowl combine turkey, ¼ cup chutney, salt, pepper and hot pepper sauce. Shape turkey mixture into 4 burgers, approximately 3½ inches in diameter. Grill turkey burgers 5 to 6 minutes per side until 160°F is reached on meat thermometer and meat is no longer pink in center.

3. In small bowl combine yogurt, curry powder and remaining ¼ cup chutney.

4. To serve, place burgers on bottom halves of buns; spoon yogurt mixture over burgers and cover with top halves of buns.

Makes 4 servings

Favorite recipe from **National Turkey Federation**

Southwest Pesto Burgers, continued

Makes 4 servings

Favorite recipe from **National Turkey Federation**

Bacon Burgers

    1 pound lean ground beef
    4 crisply cooked bacon slices, crumbled
  1½ teaspoons chopped fresh thyme *or* ½ teaspoon dried
       thyme leaves
    ½ teaspoon salt
      Dash black pepper
    4 slices Swiss cheese

Preheat grill.

Combine ground beef, bacon, thyme, salt and pepper in medium bowl; mix lightly. Shape into four patties.

Grill 4 minutes; turn. Top with cheese. Continue grilling 2 minutes or until no longer pink in center (160°F).

Makes 4 servings

Teriyaki Turkey Burgers

    1 pound ground turkey
   ⅓ cup LAWRY'S® Teriyaki Marinade with Pineapple Juice
   3 tablespoons thinly sliced green onions
   ¼ cup crushed pineapple, drained
   ½ teaspoon LAWRY'S® Garlic Powder with Parsley

In medium bowl, combine all ingredients; mix well. Form into 4 patties (mixture will be moist). Grill or broil 5 inches from heat source 3 to 5 minutes on each side or until no longer pink in center (160°F).

Makes 4 servings

Serving Suggestion: Excellent on onion buns with lettuce, red onion and pineapple slices.

Velveeta® Stuffed Burgers

Prep Time: 15 minutes
Grill Time: 18 minutes

1½ pounds lean ground beef
½ pound (8 ounces) **VELVEETA® Pasteurized Prepared Cheese Product or VELVEETA® LIGHT Pasteurized Prepared Cheese Product, cut up**
4 hamburger buns, split, toasted
Lettuce leaves, tomato slices, red onion slices

SHAPE meat into 8 thin patties. Top 4 patties each with ¼ of VELVEETA. Top with remaining 4 patties; pinch edges together to seal.

PLACE on grill over medium coals. Grill 7 to 9 minutes on each side or until cooked through (160°F). Serve patties in buns topped with lettuce, tomato and onion.   *Makes 4 sandwiches*

Wholesome Tip

Substitute ½ pound (8 ounces) VELVEETA Mexican Pasteurized Prepared Cheese Product with Jalapeno Peppers for VELVEETA Pasteurized Prepared Cheese Product.

Mississippi Barbecue Burgers

Prep Time: 30 minutes
Grill Time: 10 to 15 minutes

    1 cup FRANK'S® or SNOWFLOSS® Kraut, drained
    ⅓ cup cranberry sauce
    ¼ cup MISSISSIPPI® Barbecue Sauce
    2 tablespoons brown sugar
    1 egg, slightly beaten
    1 envelope dried onion soup mix
    ¼ cup water
    1 pound ground beef
    4 onion or sesame seed hamburger rolls, split, lightly
       toasted

1. Mix kraut, cranberry sauce, barbecue sauce and brown sugar in small saucepan; bring to a boil. Reduce heat and simmer about 15 minutes, stirring occasionally.

2. Meanwhile, in medium bowl combine egg, soup mix and water. Let stand 5 minutes. Add ground beef; mix thoroughly. Form into 4 patties.

3. Barbecue patties over mesquite or charcoal until no longer pink in center (160°F). Serve on toasted rolls topped with kraut mixture.

Makes 4 servings

Grilled Jalapeño Turkey Burgers

Prep Time: 15 minutes

- 1 package (1¼ pounds) BUTTERBALL® Lean Fresh Ground Turkey
- ¼ cup chopped green onions
- 2 tablespoons chopped pickled jalapeño peppers or mild green chilies
- 1 clove garlic, minced
- 1 teaspoon Worcestershire sauce
- ½ teaspoon salt
- ⅛ teaspoon black pepper

Prepare grill for medium-direct-heat cooking. Lightly spray unheated grill rack with nonstick cooking spray. Combine all ingredients in large bowl; mix well. Form into six large patties. Grill 6 minutes on each side or until meat is no longer pink in center. Serve with your favorite condiments.   *Makes 6 burgers*

Ranch Burgers

1¼ **pounds lean ground beef**
¾ **cup prepared HIDDEN VALLEY® The Original Ranch®**
    Dressing
¾ **cup dry bread crumbs**
¼ **cup minced onions**
 1 **teaspoon salt**
¼ **teaspoon black pepper**
    Sesame seed buns
    Lettuce, tomato slices and red onion slices (optional)
    Additional HIDDEN VALLEY® The Original Ranch®
    Dressing

In large bowl, combine beef, salad dressing, bread crumbs, onions, salt and pepper. Shape into 6 patties. Grill over medium-hot coals 5 to 6 minutes until no longer pink in center (160°F). Place on sesame seed buns with lettuce, tomato and red onion slices, if desired. Serve with a generous amount of additional salad dressing. *Makes 6 servings*

SWEET DILL
Pickles

Mushroom-Stuffed Pork Burgers

Prep Time: 15 minutes
Cook Time: 15 minutes

- ¾ **cup thinly sliced fresh mushrooms**
- ¼ **cup thinly sliced green onion**
- 1 **clove garlic, minced**
- 2 **teaspoons butter or margarine**
- 1½ **pounds lean ground pork**
- 1 **teaspoon Dijon-style mustard**
- 1 **teaspoon Worcestershire sauce**
- ¼ **teaspoon salt**
- ⅛ **teaspoon freshly ground pepper**

In skillet, sauté mushrooms, onion and garlic in butter until tender, about 2 minutes; set aside.

Combine ground pork, mustard, Worcestershire sauce, salt and pepper; mix well. Shape into 12 patties, about 4 inches in diameter. Spoon mushroom mixture onto center of 6 patties. Spread to within ½ inch of edges. Top with remaining 6 patties; seal edges.

Place patties on grill about 6 inches over medium coals. Grill 10 to 15 minutes or until no longer pink in center, turning once. Serve on buns, if desired. *Makes 6 servings*

Favorite recipe from **National Pork Board**

Grilled Salmon Burgers

1 pound fresh boneless, skinless salmon
2 tablespoons sliced green onions
1 teaspoon LAWRY'S® Garlic Pepper
½ teaspoon LAWRY'S® Seasoned Salt
2 tablespoons LAWRY'S® Citrus Grill Marinade with
    Orange Juice

In food processor, combine all ingredients; process on pulse
setting until salmon is well minced and mixed. Form into
4 patties. Broil or grill, 4 to 5 inches from heat source, 3 to
4 minutes on each side, or until cooked through.

Makes 4 servings

Serving Suggestion: Serve on warm toasted hamburger buns.

Cheesy Spinach Burgers

**1 envelope LIPTON® RECIPE SECRETS® Onion Soup
    Mix**
2 pounds ground beef
**1 package (10 ounces) frozen chopped spinach, thawed
    and squeezed dry**
**1 cup shredded mozzarella or Cheddar cheese (about
    4 ounces)**

1. In large bowl, combine all ingredients; shape into 8 patties.

2. Grill or broil until no longer pink in center (160°F). Serve, if
desired, on hamburger buns.   *Makes 8 servings*

Blackened Burgers

1 pound ground beef
5 tablespoons A.1.® Steak Sauce, divided
4 teaspoons coarsely cracked black pepper, divided
4 kaiser rolls, split
4 tomato slices

In medium bowl, combine ground beef, 3 tablespoons steak sauce and 1 teaspoon pepper; shape mixture into 4 patties. Brush patties with remaining steak sauce; coat with remaining pepper.

Grill burgers over medium heat for 5 minutes on each side or until no longer pink in center (160°F). Top each roll bottom with burger, tomato slice and roll top. Serve immediately.

Makes 4 servings

Wholesome Tip

For an extra kick in these burgers, substitute A.1.® BOLD & SPICY Steak Sauce for the A.1.® Steak Sauce.

All-American Turkey Burgers

　1 pound ground turkey
½ cup chopped onion
¼ cup ketchup
　1 clove garlic, minced
⅛ teaspoon pepper
　4 kaiser rolls, sliced
　4 leaves lettuce
　4 slices tomato
　4 slices onion

1. Preheat charcoal grill for direct-heat cooking.

2. In medium bowl combine turkey, onion, ketchup, garlic and pepper. Shape turkey mixture into 4 burgers, approximately 3½ inches in diameter.

3. Grill burgers 5 to 6 minutes per side until 160°F is reached on meat thermometer and meat is no longer pink in center.

4. To serve, place each burger on bottom half of roll; top with lettuce, tomato and onion and top half of roll.

Makes 4 servings

Favorite recipe from **National Turkey Federation**

Garden Garlic Burgers

1½ pounds ground beef or turkey
1 envelope LIPTON® RECIPE SECRETS® Onion Soup Mix*
2 small carrots, finely shredded
1 small zucchini, shredded
1 egg, slightly beaten
¼ cup plain dry bread crumbs

*Also terrific with LIPTON® RECIPE SECRETS® Savory Herb with Garlic, Golden Herb with Mushroom or Onion Mushroom Soup Mix.

1. In large bowl, combine all ingredients; shape into 6 patties.

2. Grill or broil until no longer pink in center (160°F). Serve, if desired, on hamburger buns or whole wheat rolls.

Makes 6 servings

Carolina-Style Barbecue Chicken

2 pounds boneless skinless chicken breast halves
¾ cup packed light brown sugar, divided
¾ cup *French's*® Classic Yellow® Mustard
½ cup cider vinegar
¼ cup *Frank's*® *RedHot*® Cayenne Pepper Sauce
2 tablespoons vegetable oil
2 tablespoons *French's*® Worcestershire Sauce
½ teaspoon salt
¼ teaspoon black pepper

1. Place chicken in large resealable plastic food storage bag. Combine ½ cup brown sugar, mustard, vinegar, **Frank's RedHot** Sauce, oil, Worcestershire, salt and pepper in 4-cup measure; mix well. Pour 1 cup mustard mixture over chicken. Seal bag; marinate in refrigerator 1 hour or overnight.

2. Pour remaining mustard mixture into small saucepan. Stir in remaining ¼ cup sugar. Bring to a boil. Reduce heat; simmer 5 minutes or until sugar dissolves and mixture thickens slightly, stirring often. Reserve for serving sauce.

3. Place chicken on well-oiled grid, reserving marinade. Grill over high heat 10 to 15 minutes or until chicken is no longer pink in center, turning and basting once with marinade. *Do not baste during last 5 minutes of cooking.* Discard any remaining marinade. Serve chicken with reserved sauce.

Makes 8 servings

Carolina-Style Barbecue Chicken and
Herbed Corn on the Cob (page 33)

Lime-Mustard Marinated Chicken

**2 boneless skinless chicken breast halves (about
    3 ounces each)**
¼ cup fresh lime juice
3 tablespoons honey mustard, divided
2 teaspoons olive oil
¼ teaspoon ground cumin
⅛ teaspoon garlic powder
⅛ teaspoon ground red pepper
**¾ cup plus 2 tablespoons fat-free, reduced-sodium
    chicken broth, divided**
¼ cup uncooked rice
1 cup broccoli florets
⅓ cup matchstick carrots

1. Rinse chicken. Pat dry with paper towels. Place in resealable plastic food storage bag. Whisk together lime juice, 2 tablespoons mustard, olive oil, cumin, garlic powder and red pepper. Pour over chicken. Seal bag. Marinate in refrigerator 2 hours.

2. Combine ¾ cup chicken broth, rice and remaining 1 tablespoon mustard in small saucepan. Bring to a boil. Reduce heat and simmer, covered, 12 minutes or until rice is almost tender. Stir in broccoli, carrots and remaining 2 tablespoons chicken broth. Cook, covered, 2 to 3 minutes more or until vegetables are crisp-tender and rice is tender.

3. Meanwhile, drain chicken; discard marinade. Prepare grill for direct grilling. Grill chicken over medium coals 10 to 13 minutes or until no longer pink in center. Serve chicken with rice mixture.

Makes 2 servings

Tequila Sunrise Chicken

4 boneless, skinless chicken breasts
⅓ cup lime juice
2 tablespoons KNOTT'S® Jalapeño Jelly
2 tablespoons chopped fresh cilantro
2 tablespoons tequila
2 tablespoons olive oil
1 teaspoon minced fresh garlic
¼ teaspoon salt
¼ teaspoon pepper

1. Rinse and pat dry chicken. Arrange chicken in 8×8×2-inch baking dish; set aside.

2. In small bowl, combine *remaining* ingredients. Pour half the marinade over chicken and reserve *remaining* marinade for basting. Refrigerate chicken 2 to 8 hours.

3. Place chicken on grill over hot coals. Grill chicken until no longer pink and juices run clear, basting frequently with reserved marinade. *Makes 4 servings*

Spicy Orange Oriental Chicken Breast

¼ **cup CRISCO® Oil***
1 **orange, juiced (about ⅓ cup)**
1 **tablespoon orange marmalade**
1 **teaspoon minced fresh ginger** *or* ½ **teaspoon ground**
    ginger
1 **teaspoon grated orange peel**
1 **teaspoon soy sauce**
    Dash salt and pepper
6 **boneless skinless chicken breast halves (about**
    1½ pounds)

Use your favorite Crisco Oil product.

1. Combine oil, orange juice, marmalade, ginger, orange peel, soy sauce, salt and pepper in shallow baking dish. Stir well. Add chicken. Turn to coat. Refrigerate 30 to 45 minutes, turning once.

2. Prepare grill or heat broiler.

3. Remove chicken from orange juice marinade; discard marinade. Grill or broil 3 to 5 minutes per side or until chicken is no longer pink in center.   *Makes 6 servings*

Chicken Teriyaki Kabobs

4 boneless, skinless chicken breast halves (about 1 pound), cut into 1-inch cubes
2 medium zucchini, cut into ½-inch-thick slices
1 medium-sized green bell pepper, cut into 1-inch squares
1 small red onion, cut into ½-inch cubes
1 cup LAWRY'S® Teriyaki Marinade with Pineapple Juice, divided
½ teaspoon LAWRY'S® Seasoned Pepper
¼ teaspoon LAWRY'S® Garlic Powder with Parsley
Skewers

Place chicken and vegetables on skewers, alternating chicken with vegetables. Place in large shallow baking dish. Pour ¾ cup Teriyaki Marinade with Pineapple Juice over kabobs. Turn kabobs over to coat all sides. Cover dish. Refrigerate at least 30 minutes, turning once. Remove skewers from marinade; discard marinade. Sprinkle skewers with Seasoned Pepper and Garlic Powder with Parsley. Grill or broil skewers 10 to 15 minutes or until chicken is no longer pink in center and juices run clear when cut, turning and basting often with remaining ¼ cup Teriyaki Marinade with Pineapple Juice. Do not baste during last 5 minutes of cooking.

Makes 6 servings

Serving Suggestion: Great served with steamed rice or baked potatoes.

Hint: If using wooden skewers, soak in water overnight before using to prevent scorching.

Santa Fe Grilled Chicken

Juice of 2 to 3 fresh limes (½ cup), divided
2 tablespoons vegetable oil, divided
1 package (about 3 pounds) PERDUE® Fresh Skinless
    Pick of the Chicken
Salt and black pepper to taste
1 cup fresh or frozen diced peaches
¼ cup finely chopped red onion
1 jalapeño pepper*, seeded and minced
2 cloves garlic, minced
1 teaspoon ground cumin
Chili powder

Jalapeño peppers can sting and irritate the skin; wear rubber gloves when handling peppers and do not touch eyes. Wash hands after handling peppers.

In medium-sized bowl, combine 7 tablespoons lime juice and 1 tablespoon plus 1½ teaspoons oil. Add chicken, salt and pepper; cover and marinate in the refrigerator 2 to 4 hours. Meanwhile to prepare salsa, in small bowl, combine remaining 1 tablespoon lime juice and 1½ teaspoons oil, peaches, onion, jalapeño pepper, garlic and cumin.

Prepare outdoor grill or preheat broiler. Remove chicken from marinade. Sprinkle with chili powder and place on cooking surface of grill over medium-hot coals or on broiler pan. Grill or broil 6 to 8 inches from heat source, allowing 20 to 30 minutes for breasts and 30 to 40 minutes for thighs and drumsticks, turning occasionally or until juices run clear. Serve grilled chicken with salsa. *Makes 4 to 5 servings*

Grilled Chicken with Pesto Sauce

Prep Time: 10 minutes
Cook Time: 20 minutes

- ⅓ **cup olive oil**
- ⅓ **cup loosely packed parsley sprigs**
- ⅓ **cup GREY POUPON® Dijon or COUNTRY DIJON®**
   Mustard
- ⅓ **cup pine nuts or pignoli nuts**
- 2 **tablespoons grated Parmesan cheese**
- 2 **cloves garlic**
- 1 **teaspoon dried basil leaves**
- 6 **boneless, skinless chicken thighs (1 pound)**

1. Blend oil, parsley, mustard, nuts, cheese, garlic and basil in blender or food processor until combined. Reserve ½ cup for serving.

2. Grill or broil chicken 6 inches from heat source for 15 to 20 minutes or until chicken is tender and no longer pink in center, turning once. Brush frequently with remaining pesto sauce during last 10 minutes of grilling. Serve with reserved pesto sauce.

Makes 6 servings

Barbecued Chicken

Prep Time: 25 minutes
Total Time: 1 hour

 ¼ cup CRISCO® Oil*
 1 medium onion, peeled and chopped
 ¾ cup ketchup
 ⅓ cup lemon juice or vinegar
 3 tablespoons granulated sugar
 3 tablespoons prepared mustard
 3 tablespoons Worcestershire sauce
 ½ teaspoon salt
 ½ teaspoon freshly ground black pepper
 3 pounds bone in chicken pieces *or* 4 boneless skinless
    chicken breasts flattened to even thickness

Use your favorite Crisco Oil product.

1. Heat oil in small saucepan on medium heat. Add onion. Cook
5 minutes, or until onions are soft. Add ketchup, lemon juice,
sugar, mustard, Worcestershire sauce, salt and pepper. Simmer
20 minutes, stirring occasionally.

2. Heat grill or broiler while sauce is simmering.

3. Rinse chicken. Pat dry. Place on grill on medium heat or about
8 inches from broiler. For whole bone-in pieces: Baste with sauce
after about 20 minutes. Turn chicken. Baste again after
15 minutes. Cook 5 minutes longer or until chicken is no longer
pink in center, turning and basting as needed. For boneless,
skinless breasts: Baste with sauce immediately. Turn after
5 minutes. Baste again. Grill 3 to 5 minutes, or until chicken is no
longer pink in center.**   *Makes 4 servings*

**Cooking times can vary greatly depending on size of chicken pieces and*
intensity of heat.

Chicken - 104

Blue Cheese Stuffed Chicken Breasts

Prep and Cook Time: 22 minutes

> **2 tablespoons margarine or butter, softened, divided**
> **½ cup (2 ounces) crumbled blue cheese**
> **¾ teaspoon dried thyme leaves**
> **2 whole boneless chicken breasts with skin (not split)**
> **1 tablespoon bottled or fresh lemon juice**
> **½ teaspoon paprika**

1. Prepare grill for grilling. Combine 1 tablespoon margarine, blue cheese and thyme in small bowl until blended. Season with salt and pepper.

2. Loosen skin over breast of chicken by pushing fingers between skin and meat, taking care not to tear skin. Spread blue cheese mixture under skin with rubber spatula or small spoon; massage skin to evenly spread cheese mixture.

3. Place chicken, skin side down, on grid over medium coals. Grill over covered grill 5 minutes. Meanwhile, melt remaining 1 tablespoon margarine; stir in lemon juice and paprika. Turn chicken; brush with lemon juice mixture. Grill 5 to 7 minutes more or until chicken is cooked through. Transfer chicken to carving board; cut each breast in half.   *Makes 4 servings*

Serving Suggestion: Serve with steamed new potatoes and broccoli.

Honey 'n' Spice Chicken Kabobs

1 medium green bell pepper, cut into 1-inch squares
2 boneless skinless chicken breasts, halved (about
    1¼ pounds)
1 can (8 ounces) pineapple chunks, drained
½ cup HEINZ® 57 Sauce
¼ cup honey

In small saucepan, blanch green pepper in boiling water 1 minute;
drain. Cut each chicken breast half into 4 pieces. Alternately
thread chicken, green pepper and pineapple onto skewers. In
small bowl, combine 57 Sauce and honey. Brush kabobs with
57 Sauce mixture. Grill or broil kabobs, about 6 inches from heat,
12 to 14 minutes or until chicken is tender and no longer pink in
center, turning and brushing with 57 Sauce mixture once.

Makes 4 servings

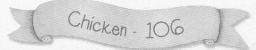

Grilled Lemon Minted Chicken Breasts

Prep Time: 30 to 40 minutes

> **3 packages BUTTERBALL® Fresh Split Chicken Breasts**
> **1 cup fresh lemon juice**
> **¼ cup chopped fresh mint leaves**
> **2 teaspoons grated lemon peel**
> **½ teaspoon red pepper flakes**

Combine lemon juice, mint leaves, lemon peel and red pepper flakes in small bowl. Grill chicken, bone side up, over hot coals 15 to 20 minutes, brushing frequently with lemon mixture. Turn and grill chicken 15 to 20 minutes longer or until internal temperature reaches 170°F and no longer pink in center. Serve grilled chicken with lemon minted couscous (see tip).

Makes 9 servings

Wholesome Tip

To prepare lemon minted couscous, prepare couscous according to package directions. Add a squeeze of fresh lemon and chopped fresh mint.

Cajun Chicken Sandwiches

Prep Time: 15 minutes
Marinate Time: 30 minutes
Cook Time: 10 minutes

> **3 tablespoons *Frank's*® *RedHot*® Cayenne Pepper Sauce,
>   divided**
> **2 tablespoons vegetable oil**
> **4 teaspoons Cajun seasoning blend, divided**
> **4 thin sliced boneless chicken breast cutlets (about
>   1 pound)**
> **1 cup mild chunky-style salsa**
>   **Lettuce**
> **4 soft rolls, split**

Combine 2 tablespoons ***Frank's RedHot*** Sauce, oil and
3 teaspoons Cajun seasoning in cup. Brush mixture onto both
sides of chicken. Cover and marinate in refrigerator 30 minutes.
Combine salsa, remaining 1 tablespoon ***Frank's RedHot*** Sauce
and 1 teaspoon Cajun seasoning in small bowl; set aside.

Place chicken on grid. Grill over medium-high coals 10 minutes or
until chicken is no longer pink in center, turning once. To serve,
layer lettuce, cooked chicken and salsa mixture on rolls, dividing
evenly.   *Makes 4 servings*

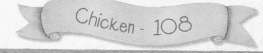

Chicken and Fruit Kabobs

1¾ cups honey
¾ cup fresh lemon juice
½ cup Dijon-style mustard
⅓ cup chopped fresh ginger
4 pounds boneless skinless chicken breasts, cut up
6 fresh plums, pitted and quartered
3 firm bananas, cut into chunks
4 cups fresh pineapple chunks (about half of medium pineapple)

Combine honey, lemon juice, mustard and ginger in small bowl; mix well. Thread chicken and fruit onto skewers, alternating chicken with fruit; brush generously with honey mixture. Place kabobs on grill about 4 inches from heat. Grill 5 minutes on each side, brushing frequently with honey mixture. Grill 10 minutes or until chicken is no longer pink in center, turning and brushing frequently with remaining honey mixture. *Makes 12 servings*

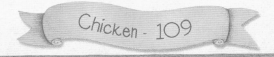

Mesquite-Grilled Chicken Quarters

**2 whole chickens (about 3½ pounds each), cut into
quarters**
2 tablespoons vegetable oil
1 small onion, chopped
1 clove garlic, minced
½ cup ketchup
2 tablespoons brown sugar
2 teaspoons chili powder
1 teaspoon dry mustard
¼ teaspoon salt
¼ teaspoon black pepper
1 can (12 ounces) beer
½ cup tomato juice
¼ cup Worcestershire sauce
1 tablespoon lemon juice

Preheat oven to 350°F. Place chickens in 1 large or 2 medium
baking pans; cover tightly with foil. Bake 30 minutes. Remove
from oven; uncover. Cool. Heat oil in 2-quart saucepan over
medium heat. Add onion and garlic; cook until onion is tender.
Combine ketchup, brown sugar, chili powder, dry mustard, salt
and pepper in medium bowl. Add remaining ingredients; whisk
until well blended. Pour into saucepan. Bring to a boil. Reduce
heat and simmer, stirring occasionally, 20 minutes or until sauce
has thickened slightly and is reduced to about 2 cups. Let cool.

Place chickens into 2 large self-sealing plastic food storage bags.
Dividing marinade equally, pour over chicken in each bag; seal
bags. Refrigerate 8 hours or overnight.

Preheat charcoal grill and grease grill rack. Remove chickens from
refrigerator and bring to room temperature. Remove chickens
from marinade and drain well; reserve marinade. Place marinade
in small saucepan; bring to a boil over medium-high heat. Boil
2 minutes; remove from heat and cool. Hook wing tips back
behind body joint on breast pieces of chicken.

continued on page 111

Mesquite-Grilled Chicken Quarters, continued

Place leg and thigh quarters on hottest part of grill 4 to 6 inches above solid bed of coals (coals should be evenly covered with gray ashes); place breast pieces on cooler edges of grill. Cook, turning occasionally, 20 to 25 minutes or until meat near thigh bone is no longer pink when slashed. Brush chicken generously with marinade during the last 10 minutes of cooking.

Makes 8 servings

Lemon-Garlic Chicken

    2 tablespoons olive oil
    2 cloves garlic, pressed
    1 teaspoon grated lemon peel
    1 teaspoon lemon juice
    ¼ teaspoon salt
    ¼ teaspoon black pepper
    4 skinless boneless chicken breast halves (about
        1 pound)

Combine oil, garlic, lemon peel, lemon juice, salt and pepper in small bowl. Brush oil mixture over both sides of chicken to coat. Lightly oil grid to prevent sticking. Grill chicken over medium KINGSFORD® Briquets 8 to 10 minutes or until chicken is no longer pink in center, turning once.

Makes 4 servings

Lime-Cilantro Marinated Chicken

　　1 cup finely chopped red onion
　　1 cup lime juice
　　½ cup red wine vinegar
　　½ cup chopped fresh cilantro
　　¼ cup vegetable oil
　　¼ cup frozen orange juice concentrate, thawed
　1¾ teaspoons LAWRY'S® Garlic Salt
　1½ teaspoons LAWRY'S® Seasoned Pepper
　　1 teaspoon chopped fresh mint
　　4 boneless, skinless chicken breast halves (about
　　　　1 pound)

In large resealable plastic food storage bag, combine all ingredients except chicken; mix well. Remove 1 cup marinade for basting. Add chicken; seal bag. Marinate in refrigerate at least 45 minutes. Remove chicken; discard used marinade. Grill or broil chicken 10 to 15 minutes or until no longer pink in center and juices run clear when cut, turning once and basting often with additional 1 cup marinade. Do not baste during last 5 minutes of cooking. Discard remaining marinade.　　　*Makes 4 servings*

Serving Suggestion: Serve with rice or warm tortillas and a green salad.

Grilled Greek Chicken

Prep Time: 10 minutes plus refrigerating
Grill Time: 50 minutes

    1 cup MIRACLE WHIP® Salad Dressing
    ½ cup chopped fresh parsley
    ¼ cup dry white wine or chicken broth
    1 lemon, sliced and halved
    2 tablespoons dried oregano leaves, crushed
    1 tablespoon garlic powder
    1 tablespoon black pepper
    2 (2½- to 3-pound) broiler-fryers, cut up

• MIX all ingredients except chicken. Pour over chicken. Cover; marinate in refrigerator at least 20 minutes. Drain marinade; discard.

• PLACE chicken on grill over medium-hot coals (coals will have slight glow). Grill, covered, 20 to 25 minutes on each side or until juices run clear.   *Makes 8 servings*

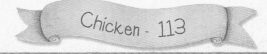

Grilled Raspberry-Thyme Chicken

4 boneless skinless chicken breast halves (4 ounces each)
3 tablespoons plus 1 teaspoon red raspberry preserves, divided
1 tablespoon lemon juice
2 teaspoons reduced-sodium soy sauce, divided
¾ teaspoon grated lemon peel
¾ teaspoon dried thyme leaves
¾ pound fresh spinach, washed, stemmed and torn
1 small cantaloupe, thinly sliced and peeled
6 ounces fresh raspberries
2 tablespoons rice wine vinegar
2 teaspoons canola or vegetable oil

Place chicken in small resealable plastic food storage bag. Blend 2 tablespoons raspberry preserves, lemon juice, 1 teaspoon soy sauce, lemon peel and thyme in small cup; pour into bag over chicken. Seal bag securely; turn bag several times to coat chicken with marinade. Refrigerate 1 hour.

Arrange spinach, cantaloupe and raspberries on serving platter. Cover with plastic wrap; refrigerate until ready to use.

For dressing, combine vinegar, remaining 4 teaspoons raspberry preserves, oil and remaining 1 teaspoon soy sauce in small jar with tight-fitting lid. Shake well; set aside.

Remove chicken from marinade; reserve marinade. Place chicken on grill 4 inches from medium-hot coals.* Grill 5 minutes. Brush top of chicken with marinade; discard remaining marinade. Turn chicken over; grill 5 to 7 minutes or until juices run clear and chicken is no longer pink in center. Cut each breast diagonally into 4 slices. Drizzle dressing over spinach and fruit; arrange chicken on top. *Makes 4 servings*

*Chicken may be broiled instead of grilled. To broil, place chicken on rack in broiler pan. Cook 4 to 5 inches from heat 6 minutes. Turn chicken over; brush with reserved marinade. Cook 6 to 8 minutes longer or until juices run clear and chicken is no longer pink in center.

Chicken Tarragon

1 package (about 3½ pounds) PERDUE® Fresh Chicken
    Breast or Leg Quarters
1 cup fresh lime juice
½ cup canola oil
1 cup chopped onions
½ cup chopped fresh tarragon *or* 4 tablespoons dried
    tarragon leaves
    Salt
    Black pepper

Place chicken in large, shallow bowl. In small bowl, combine lime juice and remaining ingredients; set aside ½ cup lime juice mixture. Pour remaining mixture over chicken; loosen skin and spoon some marinade under skin. Cover and refrigerate 1 hour or longer.

Prepare grill for cooking. Drain chicken and discard marinade. Grill chicken, uncovered, 5 to 6 inches over medium-hot coals 30 to 40 minutes or until cooked through, turning and basting frequently with reserved lime juice mixture.

Makes 4 to 6 servings

Southwest Chicken Sandwiches

¾ cup **LAWRY'S® Mesquite Marinade with Lime Juice**
½ teaspoon **LAWRY'S® Garlic Powder with Parsley**
 4 **boneless, skinless chicken breast halves (about
     1 pound)**
½ cup **chunky-style salsa**
¼ cup **mayonnaise**
 4 **sandwich rolls, split**
   Lettuce leaves
 1 **tomato, thinly sliced**
 1 **avocado, peeled, pitted and thinly sliced**

In large resealable plastic food storage bag, combine Mesquite
Marinade with Lime Juice and Garlic Powder with Parsley; mix
well. Add chicken; seal bag. Refrigerate at least 30 minutes.
Remove chicken from marinade; discard used marinade. Broil or
grill chicken breasts, 5 inches from heat source, 7 to 10 minutes
on each side or until chicken is no longer pink in center and juices
run clear when cut. In small bowl, combine salsa and
mayonnaise; spread onto cut sides of rolls. Top bottom half of
each roll with lettuce, chicken, tomato and avocado; cover with
top half of roll.   *Makes 4 servings*

Serving Suggestion: Serve with fresh fruit, chips and salsa.

Hint: For extra flavor, brush chicken with additional Mesquite
Marinade with Lime Juice while cooking.

Chicken - 116

Deviled Chicken

3 tablespoons butter or margarine
1 package (about 2¾ pounds) PERDUE® Fresh Split
    Chicken Breasts
  Salt and ground pepper to taste
2 tablespoons chili sauce or ketchup
2 tablespoons Worcestershire sauce
2 teaspoons grainy, "country-style" mustard
⅛ teaspoon ground red pepper

Prepare outdoor grill for cooking or preheat broiler. In small
saucepan over low heat, melt butter. Brush breasts with butter
and season with salt and pepper. Add chili sauce, Worcestershire
sauce, mustard and ground red pepper to butter remaining in pan;
stir to combine. Over medium heat, bring to a boil; set aside. Grill
or broil chicken 6 to 8 inches from heat source 10 to 15 minutes
per side, until nicely browned, cooked through and a meat
thermometer inserted in thickest part of breast registers 170°F.
During last 10 minutes of cooking time, baste 2 to 3 times with
butter mixture. *Makes 4 servings*

Jamaican Grilled Chicken

Prep Time: 15 minutes
Marinate Time: 1 hour
Cook Time: 45 minutes

1 whole chicken (4 pounds), cut into pieces *or* 6 whole chicken legs
1 cup coarsely chopped fresh cilantro leaves and stems
½ cup *Frank's® RedHot®* Cayenne Pepper Sauce
⅓ cup vegetable oil
6 cloves garlic, coarsely chopped
¼ cup fresh lime juice (juice of 2 limes)
1 teaspoon grated lime peel
1 teaspoon ground turmeric
1 teaspoon ground allspice

1. Loosen and pull back skin from chicken pieces. Do not remove skin. Place chicken pieces in large resealable plastic food storage bag or large glass bowl.

2. Place remaining ingredients in blender or food processor. Cover; process until smooth. Reserve ⅓ cup marinade. Pour remaining marinade over chicken pieces, turning to coat evenly. Seal bag or cover bowl; refrigerate 1 hour.

3. Prepare grill. Reposition skin on chicken pieces. Place chicken on oiled grid. Grill, over medium to medium-low coals, 45 minutes or until chicken is no longer pink near bone and juices run clear, turning and basting often with reserved marinade.

Makes 6 servings

Tutti-Fruity Chicken Kabobs

½ cup **CRISCO® Oil***
½ cup **honey**
 1 tablespoon **chopped fresh ginger** *or* 1 teaspoon **ground
   ginger**
 1 tablespoon **soy sauce**
 4 **boneless skinless chicken breast halves**
24 **(12-inch) bamboo skewers**
 1 **fresh pineapple, cut into 1-inch cubes**
 3 **oranges, peeled, quartered and cut into 1-inch pieces**
 3 **peaches, peeled, quartered and cut into 1-inch pieces**
 3 cups **steamed white rice**

Use your favorite Crisco Oil product.

1. Combine oil, honey, ginger and soy sauce in large bowl.

2. Rinse chicken; pat dry. Cut into 1-inch pieces. Place in
marinade, stirring to coat. Refrigerate 3 hours.

3. Soak bamboo skewers in water. Heat grill or broiler.

4. Thread chicken and fruit onto skewers, using 2 skewers for
each kabob. Grill or broil about 5 minutes. Baste with marinade.
Turn. Broil 5 minutes or until chicken is no longer pink in center.
Serve with steamed rice.   *Makes 6 servings (12 kabobs)*

Fresco Marinated Chicken

1 envelope **LIPTON® RECIPE SECRETS® Savory Herb with Garlic Soup Mix***
⅓ cup water
¼ cup olive or vegetable oil
1 teaspoon lemon juice or vinegar
4 boneless, skinless chicken breast halves (about 1¼ pounds)

Also terrific with LIPTON® RECIPE SECRETS® Golden Onion Soup Mix.

1. For marinade, blend all ingredients except chicken.

2. In shallow baking dish or plastic bag, pour ½ cup of the marinade over chicken. Cover, or close bag, and marinate in refrigerator, turning occasionally, up to 3 hours. Refrigerate remaining marinade.

3. Remove chicken, discarding marinade. Grill or broil chicken, turning once and brushing with refrigerated marinade until chicken is no longer pink in center. *Makes 4 servings*

Chicken - 120

Grilled Chicken Adobo

½ cup chopped onion
⅓ cup lime juice
6 cloves garlic, coarsely chopped
1 teaspoon dried oregano leaves
1 teaspoon ground cumin
½ teaspoon dried thyme leaves
¼ teaspoon ground red pepper
6 boneless skinless chicken breast halves
3 tablespoons chopped fresh cilantro

1. Combine onion, lime juice and garlic in food processor. Process until onion is finely minced. Transfer to resealable plastic food storage bag. Add oregano, cumin, thyme and red pepper; knead bag until blended. Place chicken in bag; press out air and seal. Turn to coat chicken with marinade. Refrigerate 30 minutes or up to 4 hours.

2. Spray grid with nonstick cooking spray. Prepare grill for direct cooking. Remove chicken from marinade; discard marinade. Place chicken on grid, 3 to 4 inches from medium-hot coals. Grill 5 to 7 minutes on each side or until no longer pink in center. Transfer to serving platter and sprinkle with cilantro.   *Makes 6 servings*

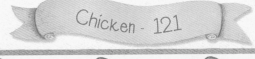

Honey-Mustard Grilled Chicken

4 boneless, skinless chicken breasts (about 4 ounces
   each)
¼ cup honey-mustard salad dressing
3 heaping tablespoons grainy Dijon mustard
2 tablespoons fresh lemon juice
1 tablespoon honey
   Salt and freshly ground black pepper, to taste

In large bowl, whisk salad dressing, mustard, lemon juice, honey,
salt and black pepper. Coat chicken halves in mixture. Cover and
marinate at least 15 minutes or overnight.

Preheat charcoal grill. Place chicken about 6 inches above
medium-hot coals. Grill chicken, turning occasionally, 10 to
20 minutes until juices run clear.   *Makes 4 servings*

Favorite recipe from **National Chicken Council**

Wholesome Tip
Serve with pasta for a quick entrée,
toss with greens topped with honey-
mustard dressing to make a salad, or
melt your favorite cheese slice over for
an easy sandwich.

Lemon-Garlic Roasted Chicken

1 chicken (3½ to 4 pounds)
   Salt and black pepper
2 tablespoons butter or margarine, softened
2 lemons, cut into halves
4 to 6 cloves garlic, peeled and left whole
5 to 6 sprigs fresh rosemary
   Garlic Sauce (recipe page 180)
   Additional rosemary sprigs and lemon wedges

Rinse chicken; pat dry with paper towels. Season with salt and pepper, then rub skin with butter. Place lemons, garlic and rosemary in cavity of chicken. Tuck wings under back and tie legs together with cotton string.

Arrange medium-low KINGSFORD® Briquets on each side of rectangular metal or foil drip pan. Pour in hot tap water to fill pan half full. Place chicken, breast side up, on grid, directly above drip pan. Grill chicken, on covered grill, about 1 hour or until meat thermometer inserted in thigh registers 175° to 180°F or until joints move easily and juices run clear when chicken is pierced. Add few briquets to both sides of fire, if necessary, to maintain constant temperature.

While chicken is cooking, prepare Garlic Sauce. When chicken is done, carefully lift from grill to wide shallow bowl so that juices from cavity run into bowl. Transfer juices to small saucepan; bring to a boil. Boil juices 2 minutes; transfer to small bowl or gravy boat. Carve chicken; serve with Garlic Sauce and cooking juices. Garnish with rosemary sprigs and lemon wedges.

Makes 4 servings

Patio Chicken Kabobs

1 cup HUNT'S® Ketchup
¼ cup LA CHOY® Lite Soy Sauce
¼ cup firmly packed brown sugar
1 teaspoon crushed red pepper flakes
4 ready-to-cook chicken kabobs (see tip)

1. In small bowl combine *all* ingredients *except* kabobs; blend well.

2. Grill kabobs over medium-hot heat, about 10 minutes.

3. Baste chicken with marinade; continue cooking and basting for 10 minutes longer or until chicken is no longer pink in center.

Makes 4 kabobs

Wholesome Tip

Ready-to-cook kabobs are available in the grocer's meat department or make your own by alternating cubed chicken pieces with vegetables on skewers.

Grilled Summer Chicken & Vegetables

1¼ cups WISH-BONE® Italian Dressing, divided*
4 chicken breast halves (about 2 pounds)
4 ears fresh or frozen corn (about 2 pounds)
2 large tomatoes, halved crosswise

*Also terrific with Wish-Bone® Robusto Italian or Lite Italian Dressing.

In large, shallow nonaluminum baking dish, pour 1 cup Italian dressing over chicken, corn and tomatoes. Cover and marinate chicken and vegetables in refrigerator, turning occasionally, 3 to 24 hours.

Remove chicken and vegetables from marinade, discarding marinade. Grill or broil chicken and corn 20 minutes, turning and brushing frequently with remaining dressing. Arrange tomato halves, cut sides up, on grill or broiler pan and continue cooking chicken and vegetables, turning and brushing occasionally with dressing, 10 minutes or until chicken is no longer pink in center and corn is tender.   *Makes 4 servings*

Fish & Shellfish

Grilled Fish with Chili-Corn Salsa

   1 cup cooked corn
   1 large tomato, seeded and diced
   ¼ cup thinly sliced green onions with tops
   ¼ cup canned diced green chilies
   1 tablespoon coarsely chopped fresh cilantro
   ⅛ teaspoon ground cumin
   1 tablespoon lime juice
   4 teaspoons olive oil, divided
   Salt and black pepper
1½ pounds firm-textured fish steaks or fillets such as
     salmon, halibut, sea bass or swordfish, each
     1 inch thick
   Cilantro sprigs for garnish

Combine corn, tomato, green onions, green chilies, cilantro, cumin, lime juice and 2 teaspoons of oil in small bowl; mix well. Add salt and pepper to taste. Let stand at room temperature 30 minutes for flavors to blend. Brush fish with remaining 2 teaspoons oil; season with salt and pepper. Preheat charcoal grill and grease grill rack. Place fish on grill 4 to 6 inches above solid bed of coals (coals should be evenly covered with grey ashes). Cook, turning once, 4 to 5 minutes on each side or until fish turns opaque and just begins to flake. Serve with salsa. Garnish with cilantro. Serve with couscous, if desired.   *Makes 4 servings*

Grilled Fish with Chili-Corn Salsa

Grilled Swordfish à l'Orange

4 swordfish, halibut or shark steaks (about 1½ pounds)
1 orange
¾ cup orange juice
1 tablespoon lemon juice
1 tablespoon sesame oil
1 tablespoon soy sauce
1 teaspoon cornstarch
Salt and black pepper to taste

Rinse swordfish and pat dry with paper towels. Grate enough orange peel to measure 1 teaspoon; set aside. Peel orange and cut into sections; set aside. Combine orange juice, lemon juice, oil and soy sauce in small bowl. Pour half of orange juice mixture into shallow glass dish. Add ½ teaspoon grated orange peel to orange juice mixture. Place fish in dish; turn to coat in mixture. Cover and allow to marinate in refrigerator up to 1 hour.

Place remaining half of orange juice mixture in small saucepan. Stir in cornstarch and remaining ½ teaspoon orange peel. Heat over medium-high heat, stirring constantly, 3 to 5 minutes or until sauce thickens; set aside.

Remove fish from marinade; discard remaining marinade. Lightly sprinkle fish with salt and pepper. Grill over medium coals 3 to 4 minutes per side or until fish is opaque and flakes easily when tested with fork. Top with reserved orange sections and orange sauce. Serve immediately.

Makes 4 servings

Mesquite-Grilled Salmon Fillets

2 tablespoons olive oil
1 clove garlic, minced
2 tablespoons lemon juice
1 teaspoon grated lemon peel
½ teaspoon dried dill weed
½ teaspoon dried thyme leaves
¼ teaspoon salt
¼ teaspoon black pepper
4 salmon fillets, ¾ to 1 inch thick (about 5 ounces each)

Cover 1 cup mesquite chips with cold water; soak 20 to
30 minutes. Prepare grill for direct cooking.

Combine oil and garlic in small microwavable bowl. Microwave
at HIGH 1 minute or until garlic is tender. Add lemon juice,
lemon peel, dill, thyme, salt and pepper; whisk until blended.
Brush skinless sides of salmon with half of lemon mixture.

Drain mesquite chips; sprinkle chips over coals. Place salmon,
skin side up, on grid. Grill, covered, over medium-high heat
4 to 5 minutes; turn and brush with remaining lemon mixture.
Grill 4 to 5 minutes or until salmon flakes easily when tested
with fork.   *Makes 4 servings*

Provençal Grilled Tuna Salad

4 (5- to 6-ounce) tuna steaks, ¾ to 1 inch thick
3 tablespoons white wine or fish broth
3 tablespoons olive oil
2 tablespoons red wine vinegar
½ teaspoon chopped fresh rosemary *or* ¼ teaspoon dried
    rosemary
½ teaspoon black pepper
⅛ teaspoon salt
1 clove garlic, minced
    Vegetable cooking spray
6 cups packed, torn salad greens
1 cup halved cherry tomatoes

Measure thickness of fish to determine cooking time; place in glass dish. To make vinaigrette, combine wine, oil, vinegar, rosemary, pepper and salt in jar with tight-fitting lid. Shake well. Pour 2 tablespoons vinaigrette over fish; add garlic and turn to coat. Marinate 15 to 30 minutes, turning once. Reserve remaining vinaigrette for salad dressing.

Coat grill rack with cooking spray and place on grill to heat 1 minute. Place tuna on grill 4 to 6 inches over hot coals. Cover with lid or tent with foil. Cook, turning once, just until tuna begins to flake easily when tested with fork, about 7 minutes. Discard marinade.

Meanwhile, arrange salad greens on 4 plates. Place hot tuna on greens and add cherry tomatoes. Shake remaining vinaigrette and drizzle over salads. *Makes 4 servings*

Note: Halibut, swordfish or shark can be substituted for tuna.

Favorite recipe from **National Fisheries Institute**

Teriyaki Trout

4 whole trout (about 2 pounds)
¾ cup LAWRY'S® Teriyaki Marinade with Pineapple Juice
½ cup sliced green onions
2 medium lemons, sliced
  Chopped fresh parsley (optional)

Brush the inside and outside of each trout with Teriyaki Marinade with Pineapple Juice; stuff with green onions and lemon slices. Place in shallow glass dish. Remove ¼ cup Teriyaki Marinade with Pineapple Juice for basting. Pour ½ cup Teriyaki Marinade with Pineapple Juice over trout; cover dish. Marinate in refrigerator at least 30 minutes. Remove trout; discard used marinade. Place trout in oiled hinged wire grill basket; brush with reserved ¼ cup Teriyaki Marinade with Pineapple Juice. Grill, 4 to 5 inches from heat source over medium-hot coals, 10 minutes or until trout flakes easily with fork, turning and brushing occasionally with reserved marinade. *Do not baste during last 5 minutes of cooking.* Discard used marinade. Sprinkle with parsley, if desired.   *Makes 4 servings*

Wholesome Tip

For a delicious side dish, cook sliced bell pepper, onion and zucchini brushed with vegetable oil on grill with trout.

Grilled Fish with Roasted Jalapeño Rub

    3 tablespoons chopped cilantro
    2 tablespoons lime juice
    1 tablespoon minced garlic
    1 tablespoon minced fresh ginger
    1 tablespoon minced roasted jalapeño peppers* (see tip)
1½ pounds firm white fish fillets, such as orange roughy
      or red snapper
    Lime wedges

Jalapeño peppers can sting and irritate the skin; wear rubber gloves when handling peppers and do not touch eyes. Wash hands after handling peppers.

Combine cilantro, lime juice, garlic, ginger and peppers in small bowl. Lightly oil grid to prevent sticking. Grill fish on covered grill over hot KINGSFORD® Briquets 5 minutes. Turn; spread cilantro mixture on fish. Grill 3 to 5 minutes longer or until fish flakes easily when tested with fork. Serve with lime wedges.

Makes 4 servings

Wholesome Tip

To roast peppers, place them on an uncovered grill over hot coals. Grill until skin is blistered, turning frequently. Remove from grill and place peppers in large resealable plastic food storage bag for 15 minutes. Remove skins. Seed peppers, if desired, and cut them into thin slices.

Halibut Kabobs

1 cup LAWRY'S® Lemon Pepper Marinade with Lemon
    Juice, divided
1 pound halibut steaks, cut into 1-inch cubes
1 green bell pepper, cut into chunks
12 cherry tomatoes
12 mushrooms, stems removed
    Skewers

In large resealable plastic food storage bag, combine ¾ cup Lemon
Pepper Marinade with Lemon Juice and halibut; seal bag.
Marinate in refrigerator at least 30 minutes. Remove halibut;
discard used marinade. Alternately thread halibut, bell pepper,
tomatoes and mushrooms onto skewers. Grill or broil skewers
8 to 10 minutes or until fish flakes easily when tested with fork,
turning once and basting often with additional ¼ cup Lemon
Pepper Marinade with Lemon Juice. *Do not baste during last
5 minutes of cooking.* Discard remaining marinade.

Makes 4 servings

Serving Suggestion: Serve with hot cooked orzo pasta or rice pilaf.

Variation: Lawry's® Herb & Garlic Marinade with Lemon Juice can
be substituted for Lemon Pepper Marinade with Lemon Juice.

Hint: If using wooden skewers, soak in water overnight before
using to prevent scorching.

Grilled Swordfish with Mango Salsa

2 pounds swordfish steaks, cut 1 inch thick
1½ cups pineapple juice, divided
1 teaspoon minced fresh ginger, divided
2 medium mangoes, peeled and coarsely chopped
4 kiwifruit, peeled and chopped
1 cup pineapple chunks
1 tablespoon brown sugar
1 tablespoon grated orange peel

1. Place fish steaks in resealable plastic food storage bag. Combine ¾ cup pineapple juice and ½ teaspoon ginger in small bowl. Pour over fish, turning to coat. Seal bag. Marinate in refrigerator about 2 hours, turning several times.

2. Combine remaining ¾ cup pineapple juice, ½ teaspoon ginger, mangoes, kiwifruit, pineapple chunks, brown sugar and orange peel in medium bowl. Cover; refrigerate.

3. Remove fish from marinade; discard marinade. Arrange fish on rack of broiler pan sprayed with nonstick cooking spray. Broil, 4 inches from heat, 5 minutes on each side or until fish begins to flake easily when tested with fork. Or, grill fish, on covered grill over medium-hot coals, 5 minutes on each side or until fish begins to flake easily when tested with fork. Serve with mango salsa and rice, if desired.   *Makes 6 servings*

Honey Barbecued Halibut

PAM® No-Stick Cooking Spray
2 pounds halibut steaks
½ cup HUNT'S® Original Barbecue Sauce
2 tablespoons honey
1 tablespoon WESSON® Vegetable Oil
½ teaspoon red wine vinegar

1. Spray a 9×9×2-inch baking pan with cooking spray. Place fish in baking pan.

2. In a small bowl, combine *remaining* ingredients.

3. Pour ⅔ *marinade* over fish. Set aside *remaining* marinade. Turn fish to coat evenly. Cover and marinate in refrigerator at least 2 hours.

4. Remove fish from marinade; discard used marinade.

5. Cook over hot coals or a preheated broiler 4 minutes per side basting occasionally with *remaining* marinade.

Makes 8 (5-ounce) servings

Grilled Herb Trout

6 whole cleaned trout (each at least 10 ounces), head
    removed if desired, boned and butterflied
  Salt and black pepper
6 bacon slices
6 sprigs dill or tarragon
1 or 2 medium onions, cut into wedges
  Lemon wedges
  Dill or tarragon sprigs for garnish

Rinse fish; pat dry with paper towels. Season lightly with salt and
pepper. Place 1 slice of bacon and 1 herb sprig in the cavity of
each trout; close fish. (There's no need to tie the fish; it will
remain closed during cooking.) Place fish in a fish basket, if
desired.

Oil hot grid to help prevent sticking. Grill fish, on covered grill,
over medium-hot KINGSFORD® Briquets, 8 to 12 minutes.
Halfway through cooking time, turn fish and add onions to grill.
Continue grilling until fish turns from transparent to opaque
throughout. Serve with lemon. (The bacon does not become
crispy; it flavors and bastes the fish during cooking. It can be
removed, if desired, just before serving.) Garnish with dill sprigs.

Makes 6 servings

Teriyaki Salmon Steaks

½ cup **LAWRY'S® Teriyaki Marinade with Pineapple Juice**
¼ **cup sherry**
2 **tablespoons orange juice**
1 **tablespoon Dijon-style mustard**
4 **salmon steaks (about 2 pounds)**
1 **large tomato, chopped**
½ **cup thinly sliced green onion**

In large resealable plastic food storage bag, combine Teriyaki Marinade with Pineapple Juice, sherry, orange juice and mustard; mix well. Remove ¼ cup marinade for basting. Add salmon; seal bag. Marinate in refrigerator at least 40 minutes, turning occasionally. In small bowl, combine tomato and green onion; set aside. Remove salmon; discard used marinade. Broil or grill, 4 inches from heat source, 3 to 5 minutes, brushing once with additional ¼ cup marinade; turning salmon once. Spoon vegetables over salmon; broil or grill 3 to 5 minutes longer or until thickest part of salmon flakes easily with fork. *Do not baste during last 5 minutes of cooking.* Discard any remaining marinade. Garnish as desired.   *Makes 4 servings*

Serving Suggestion: Delicious served with cooked julienne potatoes or hot fluffy rice.

Grilled Salmon with Cilantro Butter

    1 clove garlic, peeled
    ⅓ cup fresh cilantro leaves
    ¼ cup butter or margarine, softened
    ½ teaspoon grated lime or lemon peel
    ¼ teaspoon black pepper
    4 salmon fillets (about 6 ounces each)
     Salt (optional)
     Lime or lemon wedges

1. Drop garlic through feed tube of food processor with motor
running. Add cilantro leaves; process until cilantro is coarsely
chopped. Add butter, lime peel and pepper; process until well
combined and cilantro is finely chopped.

2. Place butter mixture on sheet of waxed paper. Using waxed
paper as a guide, roll mixture back and forth into 1-inch-diameter
log, 2 inches long. Wrap waxed paper around butter mixture to
seal; refrigerate until firm, about 30 minutes.

3. Meanwhile, prepare grill for direct cooking.

4. Lightly sprinkle salmon with salt. Place salmon, skin side
down, on grid. Grill salmon, on covered grill, over medium coals
8 to 10 minutes or until salmon flakes easily when tested with
fork.

5. Transfer salmon to serving plates. Cut butter log crosswise into
8 slices; top each fillet with 2 slices. Serve with lime or lemon
wedges.   *Makes 4 servings*

Moroccan Swordfish

4 swordfish steaks (4 ounces each), about 1 inch thick
1 tablespoon fresh lemon juice
1 tablespoon apple cider vinegar
2½ teaspoons garlic-flavored vegetable oil
1 teaspoon ground ginger
1 teaspoon paprika
½ teaspoon ground cumin
½ teaspoon hot chili oil
¼ teaspoon salt
¼ teaspoon ground coriander
⅛ teaspoon black pepper
2⅔ cups prepared couscous

1. Place swordfish in single layer in medium shallow dish. Combine lemon juice, vinegar, garlic-flavored oil, ginger, paprika, cumin, chili oil, salt, coriander and pepper in small bowl; pour over swordfish and turn to coat both sides. Cover and refrigerate 40 minutes, turning once.

2. Discard marinade; grill swordfish on uncovered grill over medium-hot coals 8 to 10 minutes or until swordfish is opaque and flakes easily when tested with fork, turning once. Serve with couscous.   *Makes 4 servings*

Vegetable-Topped Fish Pouches

4 firm fish fillets, such as flounder, cod or halibut (about 1 pound)
1 carrot, cut into very thin strips
1 rib celery, cut into very thin strips
1 medium red onion, cut into thin wedges
1 medium zucchini or yellow squash, sliced
8 mushrooms, sliced
½ cup (about 2 ounces) shredded Swiss cheese
½ cup WISH-BONE® Italian Dressing*

*Also terrific with Wish-Bone® Robusto Italian or Just 2 Good Italian Dressing.

On four 18×9-inch pieces heavy-duty aluminum foil, divide fish equally. Evenly top with vegetables, then cheese. Drizzle with Italian dressing. Wrap foil loosely around fillets and vegetables, sealing edges airtight with double fold. Let stand to marinate 15 minutes. Grill or broil pouches, seam sides up, 15 minutes or until fish flakes easily with fork.   *Makes 4 servings*

"Grilled" Tuna with Vegetables in Herb Butter

    4 pieces heavy-duty aluminum foil, each 12×18 inches
    1 (7-ounce) pouch of STARKIST® Premium Albacore or
        Chunk Light Tuna
    1 cup slivered red or green bell pepper
    1 cup slivered yellow squash or zucchini
    1 cup pea pods, cut crosswise into halves
    1 cup slivered carrots
    4 green onions, cut into 2-inch slices
        Salt and black pepper to taste (optional)

Herb Butter
    3 tablespoons butter or margarine, melted
    1 tablespoon lemon or lime juice
    1 clove garlic, minced
    2 teaspoons dried tarragon leaves, crushed
    1 teaspoon dried dill weed

On each piece of foil, mound tuna, bell pepper, squash, pea pods, carrots and onions. Sprinkle with salt and black pepper.

For Herb Butter, in small bowl stir together butter, lemon juice, garlic, tarragon and dill. Drizzle over tuna and vegetables. Fold edges of each foil square together to make packets.

To grill
Place foil packets about 4 inches above hot coals. Grill for 10 to 12 minutes or until heated through, turning packets over halfway through grill time.

To bake
Place foil packets on baking sheet. Bake in preheated 450°F oven for 15 to 20 minutes or until heated through.

To serve
Cut an "X" on top of each packet; peel back foil.

Makes 4 servings

Fish in Foil

1 (8-ounce) can stewed tomatoes
⅓ cup A.1.® BOLD & SPICY Steak Sauce
1 clove garlic, minced
4 (4-ounce) firm fish fillets
2 cups frozen mixed vegetables

In small bowl, combine stewed tomatoes, steak sauce and garlic; set aside.

Place each fish fillet in center of heavy duty or double thickness foil; top each with ½ cup mixed vegetables and ¼ cup steak sauce mixture. Wrap foil securely.

Grill fish packets over medium heat for 8 to 10 minutes or until fish flakes easily with fork. Serve immediately.

Makes 4 servings

Wholesome Tip

Cooking food in foil is a great way for an easy to clean-up meal. After you have eaten, there are no dishes to clean!

Tuna Kabobs with Red Pepper Relish

Prep Time: 25 minutes
Marinate Time: 15 minutes
Cook Time: 8 minutes

> **1 pound tuna steak, cut into 1-inch squares**
> **6 tablespoons red pepper jelly***
> **⅓ cup *French's®* Zesty Deli Mustard**
> **2 tablespoons balsamic or red wine vinegar**
> **½ teaspoon cracked black pepper**
> **¼ teaspoon salt**
> **1 red bell pepper, minced**
> **1 green onion, minced**
> **1 orange, unpeeled, cut into 1-inch pieces**
> **1 green bell pepper, cut into 1-inch pieces**

*If red pepper jelly is unavailable, combine 6 tablespoons melted apple jelly with 1 tablespoon Frank's® RedHot® Cayenne Pepper Sauce. Mix well.

1. Place tuna in large resealable plastic food storage bag. Combine jelly, mustard, vinegar, black pepper and salt in 1-cup measure. Pour ½ cup jelly marinade over tuna. Seal bag; marinate in refrigerator 15 minutes.

2. Combine remaining jelly marinade, red bell pepper and onion in small serving bowl. Reserve for relish.

3. Alternately thread tuna, orange and green bell pepper onto 4 (12-inch) metal skewers. Place skewers on oiled grid. Grill over medium-low heat 8 to 10 minutes or until fish is opaque, but slightly soft in center, turning and basting halfway with marinade.** Serve with red pepper relish.   *Makes 4 servings*

**Tuna becomes dry and tough if overcooked. Watch carefully while grilling.

Grilled Tuna with Salsa Salad

Prep Time: 5 minutes
Cook Time: 5 to 6 minutes

**1 bag (16 ounces) BIRDS EYE® frozen Farm Fresh
  Mixtures Broccoli, Corn & Red Peppers
6 to 8 green onions, sliced
1 to 2 jalapeño peppers,* finely chopped
1 can (14½ ounces) diced tomatoes with garlic and
  onion**
1 tablespoon, or to taste, lime juice or vinegar
4 tuna steaks, grilled as desired**

*Jalapeño peppers can sting and irritate the skin; wear rubber gloves
when handling peppers and do not touch eyes. Wash hands after
handling peppers.*

**Or, substitute favorite seasoned diced tomatoes.

• In large saucepan, cook vegetables according to package
directions; drain.

• In large bowl, combine vegetables, onions, peppers, tomatoes
and lime juice. Let stand 15 minutes.

• Serve vegetable mixture over tuna.   *Makes 4 servings*

Grilled Tropical Shrimp

¼ cup barbecue sauce
2 tablespoons pineapple juice or orange juice
10 ounces medium shrimp in shells
2 medium firm nectarines
1 yellow onion, cut into 8 wedges, or 6 green onions,
cut into 2-inch lengths

1. Stir together barbecue sauce and pineapple juice. Set aside.

2. Peel and devein shrimp. Cut each nectarine into 6 wedges. Thread shrimp, nectarines and onion wedges onto 4 long metal skewers.

3. Spray grill grid with nonstick cooking spray. Prepare grill for direct grilling. Grill skewers over medium coals 4 to 5 minutes or until shrimp are opaque, turning once and brushing frequently with barbecue sauce. *Makes 2 servings*

Tip: Although shrimp are high in cholesterol, they are naturally low in total fat and saturated fat, making them a good choice for a low-fat diet.

Greek Island Shrimp Pita Pockets

Prep Time: 25 minutes
Marinate Time: 15 minutes
Cook Time: 10 minutes

   1 pound large raw shrimp, shelled and deveined
   ½ cup Italian salad dressing
   3 tablespoons *French's®* Zesty Deli Mustard
   2 tablespoons fresh lemon juice
   2 teaspoons grated lemon peel
   1 teaspoon dried oregano, crumbled
   ⅛ teaspoon black pepper
   2 tablespoons reduced-fat sour cream
   1 cup chopped seeded cucumber
   1 cup chopped plum tomatoes
   2 green onions, thinly sliced
   ½ cup (2 ounces) crumbled feta cheese
   4 pita bread rounds
     Olive oil-flavored nonstick cooking spray

1. Place shrimp in large resealable plastic food storage bag. Combine dressing, mustard, lemon juice, lemon peel, oregano and pepper in 2-cup measure; mix well. Reserve 2 tablespoons marinade; pour remaining marinade over shrimp. Seal bag; marinate in refrigerator 15 minutes. Stir sour cream into reserved marinade; cover and refrigerate.

2. Toss cucumber, tomatoes, onions and feta cheese in medium bowl; set aside.

3. Thread shrimp onto 4 (6-inch) metal skewers. Place skewers on grid. Grill over medium heat 10 minutes or until shrimp are opaque, turning often. Spray pitas lightly on both sides with nonstick cooking spray; grill 1 minute or until brown on both sides.

4. To serve, cut one-third off tops of pitas; discard. Fill pitas evenly with cucumber mixture. Spoon sour cream mixture over cucumber mixture. Serve pitas with shrimp skewers.

Makes 4 servings

Grilled Prawns with Salsa Vera Cruz

Prep Time: 25 minutes
Cook Time: 6 minutes

    1 can (14½ ounces) DEL MONTE® Diced Tomatoes, drained
    1 orange, peeled and chopped
    ¼ cup sliced green onions
    ¼ cup chopped cilantro or parsley
    1 small clove garlic, crushed
    1 pound medium shrimp, peeled and deveined

1. Combine tomatoes, orange, green onions, cilantro and garlic in medium bowl.

2. Thread shrimp onto skewers; season with salt and pepper, if desired.

3. Brush grill with oil. Cook shrimp over hot coals about 3 minutes on each side or until shrimp turn pink. Top with salsa. Serve over rice and garnish, if desired.   *Makes 4 servings*

Hint: Thoroughly rinse shrimp in cold water before cooking.

Seafood Kabobs

    Nonstick cooking spray
  1 pound uncooked large shrimp, peeled and deveined
10 ounces skinless swordfish or halibut steaks, cut 1 inch
     thick
  2 tablespoons honey mustard
  2 teaspoons fresh lemon juice
  8 metal skewers (12 inches long)
  8 slices bacon (regular slice, not thick)
    Lemon wedges and fresh herbs (optional)

1. Spray grid with nonstick cooking spray. Prepare grill for direct cooking.

2. Place shrimp in shallow glass dish. Cut swordfish into 1-inch cubes; add to dish. Combine mustard and lemon juice in small bowl. Pour over shrimp mixture; toss lightly to coat.

3. Pierce one 12-inch metal skewer through 1 end of bacon slice. Add 1 piece shrimp. Pierce skewer through bacon slice again, wrapping bacon slice around 1 side of shrimp.

4. Add 1 piece swordfish. Pierce bacon slice again, wrapping bacon around opposite side of swordfish. Continue adding seafood and wrapping with bacon, pushing ingredients to middle of skewer until end of bacon slice is reached. Repeat with 7 more skewers. Brush any remaining mustard mixture over skewers.

5. Place skewers on grid. Grill, covered, over medium heat 8 to 10 minutes or until shrimp are opaque and swordfish flakes easily when tested with fork, turning halfway through grilling time. Garnish with lemon wedges and fresh herbs, if desired.

Makes 4 servings (2 kabobs per serving)

Note: Kabobs can be prepared up to 3 hours before grilling. Cover and refrigerate until ready to grill.

Grilled Scallops and Vegetables with Cilantro Sauce

1 teaspoon hot chili oil
1 teaspoon dark sesame oil
1 green onion, chopped
1 tablespoon finely chopped fresh ginger
1 cup reduced-sodium chicken broth
1 cup chopped fresh cilantro
1 pound sea scallops
2 medium zucchini, cut into ½-inch slices
2 medium yellow squash, cut into ½-inch slices
1 medium yellow onion, cut into wedges
8 large mushrooms

1. Spray cold grid with nonstick cooking spray. Preheat grill to medium-high heat. Heat chili oil and sesame oil in small saucepan over medium-low heat. Add green onion; cook about 15 seconds or just until fragrant. Add ginger; cook 1 minute.

2. Add chicken broth; bring mixture to a boil. Cook until liquid is reduced by half. Place mixture in blender or food processor with cilantro; blend until smooth. Set aside.

3. Thread scallops and vegetables onto skewers. Grill about 8 minutes per side or until scallops turn opaque. Serve hot with cilantro sauce. Garnish, if desired. *Makes 4 servings*

Beach Grill

1 cup vegetable oil
2 teaspoons LAWRY'S® Seasoned Salt
1 teaspoon LAWRY'S® Garlic Powder with Parsley
½ teaspoon hot pepper sauce (optional)
12 raw medium shrimp, peeled and deveined
12 sea scallops
1 small red onion, cut into 12 wedges
Skewers

In large resealable plastic food storage bag, combine oil, Seasoned Salt, Garlic Powder with Parsley and hot pepper sauce, if desired; mix well. Add shrimp, scallops and onion; seal bag. Marinate in refrigerator at least 1 hour. Remove shrimp, scallops and onion from marinade; discard used marinade. Alternately thread shrimp, scallops and onion onto skewers. Grill or broil skewers 4 to 6 minutes or until shrimp are pink and scallops are opaque, turning halfway through grilling time.   *Makes 6 servings*

Serving Suggestion: Serve with lime wedges and crusty French bread.

Hint: If using wooden skewers, soak in water overnight before using to prevent scorching.

Fish & Shellfish - 150

Grilled Paella

1½ to 2 pounds chicken wings or thighs
2 tablespoons plus ¼ cup extra-virgin olive oil, divided
   Salt and black pepper
1 pound garlicky sausage links, such as linguisa, chorizo
   or Italian
1 large onion, chopped
2 large red bell peppers, seeded and cut into thin strips
4 cloves garlic, minced
1 can (14 ounces) diced tomatoes, undrained
4 cups uncooked rice
1 oval disposable foil pan (about 17×13×3 inches)
16 tightly closed live mussels or clams,* scrubbed
½ pound large shrimp,* peeled and deveined with tails
   intact
1½ cups frozen peas
1 can (about 14 ounces) chicken broth
2 lemons, cut into wedges

Seafood can be omitted; add an additional 1¼ to 1½ pounds chicken.

Brush chicken with 2 tablespoons oil; season with salt and black
pepper. Grill chicken and sausage on covered grill over medium
KINGSFORD® Briquets 15 to 20 minutes or until chicken juices
run clear and sausage is no longer pink, turning every 5 minutes.
Cut sausage into 2-inch pieces.

Heat remaining ¼ cup oil in large skillet over medium-high heat.
Add onion, bell peppers and garlic; cook and stir 5 minutes or until
vegetables are tender. Add tomatoes, 1½ teaspoons salt and
½ teaspoon black pepper; cook about 8 minutes until thick, stirring
frequently. Combine onion mixture and rice in foil pan; spread
evenly. Arrange chicken, sausage, seafood and peas over rice. Bring
broth and 6 cups water to a boil in 3 quart saucepan. Place foil pan
on grid over medium KINGSFORD® briquets; immediately pour
boiling broth mixture over rice. Grill on covered grill about
20 minutes until liquid is absorbed. *Do not stir.* Cover with foil; let
stand 10 minutes. Garnish with lemon wedges.

Makes 8 to 10 servings

Fish & Shellfish - 151

Grilled Shrimp Creole

½ cup olive oil, divided
3 tablespoons balsamic or red wine vinegar
3 cloves garlic, minced and divided
1½ pounds raw large shrimp, peeled and deveined
3 tablespoons all-purpose flour
1 medium green bell pepper, coarsely chopped
1 medium onion, coarsely chopped
2 ribs celery, sliced
1 can (28 ounces) diced tomatoes, undrained
1 bay leaf
1½ teaspoons dried thyme leaves, crushed
¾ teaspoon hot pepper sauce
1 cup uncooked rice, preferably converted
1 can (about 14 ounces) chicken broth
1 can (15 ounces) red beans, rinsed and drained
¼ cup chopped fresh parsley

1. Combine ¼ cup oil, vinegar and 1 clove garlic in small bowl. Pour over shrimp; toss lightly to coat. Cover; marinate in refrigerator at least 30 minutes or up to 8 hours, turning occasionally.

2. For tomato sauce, heat remaining ¼ cup oil in large skillet over medium heat. Stir in flour. Cook and stir until flour is dark golden brown, 10 to 12 minutes. Add bell pepper, onion, celery and remaining 2 cloves garlic; cook and stir 5 minutes. Add tomatoes with juice, bay leaf, thyme and hot pepper sauce. Simmer, uncovered, 25 to 30 minutes or until sauce has thickened and vegetables are fork-tender, stirring occasionally.*

3. Meanwhile, prepare grill for direct cooking. While coals are heating, prepare rice according to package directions, substituting broth for 1¾ cups water and omitting salt. Stir in beans during last 5 minutes of cooking.

continued on page 153

4. Drain shrimp; discard marinade. Place shrimp in grill basket or thread onto metal skewers. Place grill basket or skewers on grid. Grill shrimp, on uncovered grill, over medium coals 6 to 8 minutes or until shrimp are opaque, turning halfway through grilling time.

5. Remove and discard bay leaf from tomato sauce. Arrange rice and beans on 4 serving plates; top with tomato sauce. Remove shrimp from grill basket or skewers. Arrange shrimp over tomato sauce. Sprinkle with parsley.   *Makes 4 servings*

*If desired, tomato sauce may be prepared up to 1 day ahead. Cover and refrigerate. Reheat sauce in medium saucepan over medium heat while shrimp are grilling.

Lobster Tails with Tasty Butters

Hot & Spicy Butter or Scallion Butter or Chili-Mustard Butter (recipe page 169)
4 fresh or thawed frozen lobster tails (about 5 ounces each)

Prepare grill for direct cooking. Prepare 1 butter mixture.

Rinse lobster tails in cold water. Butterfly tails by cutting lengthwise through centers of hard top shells and meat. Cut to, but not through, bottoms of shells. Press shell halves of tails apart with fingers. Brush lobster meat with butter mixture.

Place tails on grid, meat side down. Grill over medium-high heat 4 minutes. Turn tails meat side up. Brush with butter mixture and grill 4 to 5 minutes or until lobster meat turns opaque.

Heat remaining butter mixture, stirring occasionally. Serve butter sauce for dipping.   *Makes 4 servings*

Mushroom Bacon Steak Sauce

4 ounces bacon, cut into ¼-inch pieces
1 (10-ounce) package fresh mushrooms, sliced
2 tablespoons sherry cooking wine
¼ cup A.1.® Original or A.1.® BOLD & SPICY Steak
    Sauce

Cook bacon in large skillet over medium-high heat until crisp. Using slotted spoon, remove bacon. Pour off all but 2 tablespoons drippings.

Sauté mushrooms in reserved drippings in same skillet 5 minutes or until tender. Using slotted spoon, remove mushrooms. Add sherry to skillet to deglaze pan. Stir in steak sauce, reserved mushrooms and bacon; heat through. Serve warm or at room temperature with cooked steak. Garnish as desired. *Makes 1½ cups*

Mushroom Bacon Steak Sauce

Dijon-Cream Sauce

    1 can (14½ ounces) beef broth
    1 cup whipping cream
    2 tablespoons butter, softened
  1½ to 2 tablespoons Dijon mustard
    1 to 1½ tablespoons balsamic vinegar*
      Coarsely crushed black peppercorns and mustard
        seeds for garnish

*Substitute 2 teaspoons red wine vinegar plus 1 teaspoon sugar for the balsamic vinegar.

Bring beef broth and whipping cream to a boil in a saucepan. Boil gently until reduced to about 1 cup; sauce will be thick enough to coat a spoon. Remove from heat; stir in butter, a little at a time, until all the butter is melted. Stir in mustard and vinegar, adjusting amounts to taste. Sprinkle with peppercorns and mustard seeds.

Makes about 1 cup

Favorite recipe from **The Kingsford Products Company**

Golden Glaze

    ¼ cup apricot or peach preserves
    2 tablespoons spicy brown mustard*
    2 cloves garlic, minced

*Dijon mustard may be substituted. Add ¼ teaspoon hot pepper sauce to glaze.

Combine all ingredients; mix well. Store tightly covered in refrigerator up to 2 weeks. Brush on chicken, pork or shrimp before grilling or broiling. (Marinade may be easily doubled for two uses.)

Makes about ⅓ cup glaze

Chili-Lemon Sauce

¾ **cup fresh lemon juice**
1 **small onion, coarsely chopped**
3 **jalapeño peppers,* stemmed, seeded and quartered**
3 **cloves garlic, halved**

*Jalapeño peppers can sting and irritate the skin; wear rubber gloves when handling peppers and do not touch eyes. Wash hands after handling peppers.

Place all ingredients in food processor; process until smooth. Serve at room temperature.   *Makes about 1 cup*

Sage-Garlic Baste

Grated peel and juice of 1 lemon
3 **tablespoons olive oil**
2 **tablespoons minced fresh sage** *or* **1½ teaspoons rubbed sage**
2 **cloves garlic, minced**
½ **teaspoon salt**
¼ **teaspoon black pepper**

Combine all ingredients in small saucepan; cook and stir over medium heat 4 minutes. Use as baste for turkey or chicken.
                                        Makes about ½ cup

Favorite recipe from **The Kingsford Products Company**

Oriental Mustard Barbecue Sauce

Prep Time: 5 minutes

- **1 bottle (10.5 ounces) PLOCHMAN'S® Mild Yellow Mustard (about 1 cup)**
- **½ cup barbecue sauce**
- **¼ cup packed brown sugar**
- **¼ cup hoisin sauce**
- **¼ cup soy sauce**
- **2 tablespoons sesame oil**
- **2 tablespoons Chinese rice wine**
- **1 tablespoon minced fresh ginger**
- **1 clove garlic, minced**

Mix together all ingredients. Use as a condiment, or brush on chicken, seafood or steak during the last 15 minutes of cooking.

Makes 2 cups

Soy-Ginger Sauce

¼ **cup vegetable oil**
4 **tablespoons soy sauce**
½ **cup finely chopped green onion, tops included**
1 **tablespoon finely shredded gingerroot**

Combine oil, soy sauce, onion and ginger in small bowl. Marinate at least 30 minutes before serving. *Makes about ¾ cup sauce*

Favorite recipe from **National Fisheries Institute**

Citrus Marinade

½ **cup fresh lime juice**
¼ **cup vegetable oil**
2 **green onions, chopped**
1 **teaspoon dried tarragon leaves**
¼ **teaspoon garlic powder**
¼ **teaspoon black pepper**

Blend all ingredients in small bowl. Use to marinate fish before grilling. *Makes about 1 cup marinade*

Mustard-Tarragon Marinade

3 tablespoons red wine vinegar
1 tablespoon Dijon-style mustard
½ tablespoon dried tarragon
2 tablespoons olive oil

Combine first 3 ingredients in small bowl. Slowly whisk oil into mixture until slightly thickened.   *Makes about ½ cup marinade*

Favorite recipe from **Sargento® Foods Inc.**

Easy Honey Mustard Barbecue Sauce

Prep Time: 5 minutes

1 bottle (10.5 ounces) PLOCHMAN'S® Mild Yellow
   Mustard (about 1 cup)
½ cup barbecue sauce
¼ cup honey
2 tablespoons finely minced onion

Mix all ingredients in medium bowl. Use as a condiment, or brush on chicken, pork chops or seafood.   *Makes 2 cups*

Tomato Basil Butter Sauce

4 tablespoons butter or margarine, softened, divided
1½ cups chopped seeded peeled tomatoes (about 1 pound)
½ teaspoon sugar
1 clove garlic, minced
Salt and black pepper
1½ tablespoons very finely chopped fresh basil

Melt 1 tablespoon butter in a small skillet. Add tomatoes, sugar and garlic. Cook over medium-low heat, stirring frequently, until liquid evaporates and mixture thickens. Remove pan from heat; stir in remaining butter until mixture has a saucelike consistency. Season to taste with salt and pepper, then stir in basil.

Makes about 1 cup

Favorite recipe from **The Kingsford Products Company**

New Mexico Marinade

1½ cups beer
½ cup chopped fresh cilantro
3 cloves garlic
½ cup lime juice
2 teaspoons chili powder
1½ teaspoons ground cumin
1 teaspoon TABASCO® brand Pepper Sauce

Place ingredients in food processor or blender; process until well combined. Store in 1-pint covered jar in refrigerator up to 3 days. Use to marinate beef, pork or chicken in refrigerator.

Makes 2 cups

Lemon Pepper Marinade

⅔ cup A.1.® Steak Sauce
4 teaspoons grated lemon peel
1½ teaspoons coarsely ground black pepper

Combine steak sauce, lemon peel and pepper in small bowl. Use to marinate beef, fish, steak, poultry or pork for about 1 hour in the refrigerator.   *Makes about ⅔ cup*

Easy Tartar Sauce

¼ cup fat-free or reduced-fat mayonnaise
2 tablespoons sweet pickle relish
1 teaspoon lemon juice

Combine mayonnaise, relish and lemon juice in small bowl; mix well. Refrigerate until ready to serve. Serve with grilled, broiled or fried fish.   *Makes about ¼ cup*

Dilled Wine Sauce

1½ cups finely chopped onions
½ cup chopped fresh dill *or* 1 tablespoon dried dill weed
¼ cup chopped fresh tarragon *or* 1½ teaspoons dried
    tarragon leaves
1 clove garlic, peeled and cut into quarters
½ cup dry white wine
2 teaspoons extra-virgin olive oil

Combine all ingredients except oil in blender or food processor; process until smooth. Pour dill mixture into small saucepan and bring to a boil over medium heat. Reduce heat to low; simmer until reduced by half. Strain sauce into small bowl, pressing all liquid through strainer with back of spoon. Slowly whisk in oil until smooth and well blended. *Makes ½ cup*

Wholesome Tip

Use this sauce for dipping grilled fish such as salmon or white fish.

Smoky Honey Barbecue Sauce

1 cup honey
1 cup chili sauce
½ cup cider vinegar
1 teaspoon prepared mustard
1 teaspoon Worcestershire sauce
½ teaspoon pepper
½ teaspoon minced garlic
2 to 3 drops liquid smoke

Combine all ingredients except liquid smoke in medium saucepan over medium heat. Cook, stirring frequently, 20 to 30 minutes. Remove from heat; add liquid smoke to taste. Serve over grilled chicken, turkey, pork, spareribs, salmon or hamburgers.

Makes about 2 cups

Favorite recipe from **National Honey Board**

Lemon-Mustard Sauce

½ cup plain nonfat yogurt
2 tablespoons low-fat sour cream
2 tablespoons Dijon mustard
1 small clove garlic, minced
½ teaspoon grated lemon peel

Combine all ingredients in a small bowl; mix well.

Makes about ¾ cup

Spicy Orange Baste

3 tablespoons orange juice
3 tablespoons lemon juice
2 tablespoons vegetable oil
1 tablespoon grated orange peel
½ teaspoon ground ginger
½ teaspoon salt
⅛ teaspoon freshly ground pepper

Combine all ingredients in small bowl, use to baste chicken while cooking. *Makes ½ cup*

Favorite recipe from **Perdue Farms Incorporated**

Dijon Teriyaki Marinade

⅓ cup GREY POUPON® Dijon Mustard
2 tablespoons teriyaki sauce
2 tablespoons packed brown sugar

Blend all ingredients in small bowl. Use as a marinade for pork or poultry. *Makes ½ cup marinade*

Oriental Steak Marinade

1 cup A.1.® THICK & HEARTY Steak Sauce
¼ cup sherry cooking wine
¼ cup finely chopped red bell pepper
3 tablespoons firmly packed light brown sugar
3 tablespoons soy sauce
1 tablespoon Oriental sesame oil
2 cloves garlic, minced

Combine steak sauce, sherry, bell pepper, sugar, soy sauce, oil and garlic in small nonmetal bowl. Use to marinate any steak about 1 hour in refrigerator.

Remove steak from marinade; reserve marinade. Grill or broil steak to desired doneness. Meanwhile, bring reserved marinade to a boil in small saucepan over high heat; simmer 5 minutes or until thickened. Serve steak with warm sauce. *Makes 1⅔ cups*

Cowpoke Barbecue Sauce

1 teaspoon vegetable oil
¾ cup chopped green onions
3 cloves garlic, finely chopped
1 can (14½ ounces) crushed tomatoes
½ cup ketchup
¼ cup water
¼ cup orange juice
2 tablespoons cider vinegar
2 teaspoons chili sauce
   Dash Worcestershire sauce

Heat oil in medium nonstick saucepan over medium heat until hot. Add onions and garlic. Cook and stir 5 minutes or until onions are tender. Stir in remaining ingredients. Reduce heat to medium-low. Cook 15 minutes, stirring occasionally.

Makes 2 cups

Thai Marinade

½ cup A.1.® Steak Sauce
⅓ cup peanut butter
2 tablespoons soy sauce

Blend steak sauce, peanut butter and soy sauce in nonmetal container. Use to marinate beef, poultry or pork for about 1 hour in the refrigerator.

Makes 1 cup

Balsamic Marinade

2 pounds beef, pork, lamb or veal
½ cup FILIPPO BERIO® Olive Oil
½ cup balsamic vinegar
2 cloves garlic, slivered
1 teaspoon dried oregano leaves
½ teaspoon salt
½ teaspoon dried marjoram leaves
¼ teaspoon freshly ground black pepper

Place meat in shallow glass dish. In small bowl, whisk together olive oil, vinegar, garlic, oregano, salt, marjoram and pepper. Pour marinade over meat, using about ½ cup for each pound of meat. Turn to coat both sides. Cover; marinate several hours or overnight, turning meat occasionally. Remove meat; boil marinade 1 minute. Grill meat, brushing frequently with marinade.   *Makes 1 cup marinade*

Tasty Butters

Hot & Spicy Butter
⅓ cup butter or margarine, melted
1 tablespoon chopped onion
1 teaspoon dried thyme leaves
¼ teaspoon ground allspice
2 to 3 teaspoons hot pepper sauce

Scallion Butter
⅓ cup butter or margarine, melted
1 tablespoon finely chopped green onion tops
1 tablespoon lemon juice
1 teaspoon grated lemon peel
¼ teaspoon black pepper

Chili-Mustard Butter
⅓ cup butter or margarine, melted
1 tablespoon chopped onion
1 tablespoon Dijon mustard
1 teaspoon chili powder

For each butter sauce, combine ingredients in small bowl. Serve
Tasty Butters with Lobster Tails (recipe page 153) or other types
of seafood and fish.   *Makes about 1 cup each*

Maui Magic Marinade

1½ cups MAUNA LA'I® Island Guava® Juice Drink
½ cup pineapple juice
¼ cup packed brown sugar
2 large cloves garlic, finely chopped
½ teaspoon ginger
¼ teaspoon white pepper
½ cup oil

Combine Mauna La'i Island Guava Juice Drink, pineapple juice, brown sugar, garlic, ginger, pepper and oil in plastic bowl. Use with your favorite chicken, meat or fish recipes.

Makes 2½ cups

Orange Barbecue Sauce

¾ cup orange marmalade
½ cup A.1.® BOLD & SPICY Steak Sauce
½ cup GREY POUPON® Dijon Mustard
¼ cup finely chopped onion

Combine marmalade, steak sauce, mustard and onion in small bowl. Use as a baste while grilling poultry, ribs or pork.

Makes about 2 cups

Mushroom Sauce

¼ **cup milk**
2 **tablespoons cornstarch**
2 **tablespoons butter**
8 **ounces fresh white mushrooms, sliced (about 3 cups)**
⅓ **cup chopped onion**
1 **can (14 ounces) beef broth**
½ **cup water**

In small bowl, combine milk and cornstarch; set aside. In large skillet, melt butter over high heat. Add mushrooms and onion; cook and stir over medium heat until mushrooms are golden, about 10 minutes. Stir in broth and water; bring to a boil. Stir cornstarch mixture into mushroom mixture in skillet. Cook over high heat, stirring constantly, until slightly thickened, about 1 minute. *Makes 2½ cups*

Favorite recipe from **Mushroom Council**

Creamy Herb Sauce

½ cup plain yogurt
½ cup chopped peeled cucumber
1 tablespoon chopped fresh basil
1 teaspoon dried oregano leaves
½ teaspoon dried mint leaves
¼ teaspoon minced garlic
3 dashes ground red pepper

Combine all ingredients in small bowl until blended. Cover and refrigerate 1 hour before serving. Serve with grilled fish.

Makes about 1 cup

Barbecue Sauce

2 tablespoons butter
½ cup finely chopped onion
1½ cups ketchup
1 cup red currant jelly
¼ cup apple cider vinegar
3 tablespoons soy sauce
¼ teaspoon ground red pepper
¼ teaspoon ground black pepper

Melt butter in medium saucepan over medium-high heat. Add onion; cook and stir until softened. Stir in remaining ingredients. Reduce heat to medium-low; simmer 20 minutes, stirring often.

Makes about 3 cups

Chili-Spiced Marinade

½ cup A.1.® Original or A.1.® BOLD & SPICY Steak
    Sauce
½ cup ketchup
¼ cup GREY POUPON® Dijon Mustard
¼ cup red wine vinegar
¼ cup vegetable oil
2 cloves garlic, minced
1 teaspoon chili powder

In small nonmetal bowl, combine steak sauce, ketchup, mustard, vinegar, oil, garlic and chili powder. Use to marinate any steak about 1 hour in refrigerator.

Remove steak from marinade; reserve marinade. Grill or broil steak to desired doneness. Meanwhile, in small saucepan, over high heat, bring reserved marinade to a boil; simmer 5 minutes or until thickened. Serve steak with warm sauce.

Makes 1¾ cups

Southern Barbecue Sauce

3 cups ketchup
6 tablespoons cider vinegar
½ cup molasses or dark brown sugar
⅓ cup prepared mustard
2 tablespoons Worcestershire sauce
2 teaspoons LAWRY'S® Seasoned Salt
2½ to 4½ teaspoons hot pepper sauce

In small saucepan, combine all ingredients; mix well. Bring to a boil over medium-high heat. Reduce heat to low and simmer, uncovered, 5 to 10 minutes, stirring occasionally.

Makes 4 cups

Wholesome Tip

Use this sauce to baste meats or poultry while barbecuing or baking in the oven.

Fajita Marinade

½ cup lime juice *or* ¼ cup lime juice and ¼ cup tequilla
    or beer
1 tablespoon dried oregano leaves
1 tablespoon minced garlic
2 teaspoons ground cumin
2 teaspoons black pepper

Combine lime juice, oregano, garlic, cumin and black pepper in
1-cup glass measure. Use to marinate beef or chicken for fajitas.

Makes about ¾ cup

Lemon-Garlic Grilling Sauce

½ cup butter or margarine, melted
¼ cup lemon juice
1 tablespoon Worcestershire sauce
3 cloves garlic, peeled and minced
½ teaspoon TABASCO® brand Pepper Sauce
¼ teaspoon black pepper

Combine butter, lemon juice, Worcestershire sauce, garlic,
TABASCO® Sauce and black pepper in small bowl; mix well.
Brush on fish, seafood, poultry or vegetables during grilling or
broiling.

Makes ¾ cup

Peach Lemon Sauce for Chicken

2 lemons
3 fresh California peaches, peeled, halved, pitted and
quartered
3 tablespoons reduced-sodium chicken broth
Pepper
Grilled chicken

Thinly peel one lemon; reserve peel. Squeeze both lemons to measure ¼ cup juice. Combine juice and peaches in saucepan. Cover and cook 20 minutes or until peaches are tender. Meanwhile, cut reserved lemon peel into fine julienne strips; cut strips in half. Boil strips in water 7 or 8 minutes. Drain; set aside. Add cooked peaches and chicken broth to food processor or blender. Process until smooth. Stir in julienned lemon strips and pepper to taste. Serve hot over grilled chicken.

Makes 2½ cups

Favorite recipe from **California Tree Fruit Agreement**

Spicy Oriental Sauce

  2 tablespoons cornstarch
  ½ cup water
  2 tablespoons reduced-sodium soy sauce
  1 tablespoon sherry
  1 tablespoon Worcestershire sauce
  1 teaspoon curry powder

Combine ingredients in small bowl; mix well.

Makes about ¾ cup

Favorite recipe from **Riviana Foods Inc.**

Texas BBQ Sauce

  1½ cups ketchup
  ¾ cup honey
  ½ cup cider or white vinegar
  1 small onion, finely chopped
  2 tablespoons Worcestershire sauce
  1 jalapeño pepper,* seeded and minced
  1 tablespoon mustard
  1 teaspoon olive oil

*Jalapeño peppers can sting and irritate the skin; wear rubber gloves when handling peppers and do not touch eyes. Wash hands after handling peppers.

Combine all ingredients; mix well.

Makes about 3 cups

Zippy Tartar Sauce for Grilled Fish

Prep Time: 5 minutes

1 cup mayonnaise
3 tablespoons *Frank's® RedHot®* Cayenne Pepper Sauce
2 tablespoons *French's®* Zesty Deli Mustard
2 tablespoons sweet pickle relish
1 tablespoon minced capers

Combine mayonnaise, ***Frank's RedHot*** Sauce, mustard, pickle relish and capers in medium bowl. Cover and chill in refrigerator until ready to serve. Serve with grilled salmon, halibut, swordfish or tuna.

Makes 1½ cups sauce

Way-Out Western BBQ Sauce

½ cup chili sauce
¼ cup fresh lemon juice
¼ cup ketchup
2 tablespoons dry mustard
2 tablespoons brown sugar
2 tablespoons cider vinegar
2 tablespoons dark molasses
1 tablespoon Worcestershire sauce
2 teaspoons grated fresh lemon peel
½ teaspoon garlic powder
½ teaspoon ground allspice
½ teaspoon liquid smoke (optional)
¼ teaspoon hot pepper sauce

Place all ingredients in small bowl and stir until blended. Brush on meats during last 15 minutes of grilling or at beginning of grilling if cooking time is less than 15 minutes.   *Makes 10 servings*

Note: To avoid spreading bacteria from raw meats with the basting brush, pour only the sauce needed for basting into a small bowl and discard any that remains after basting.

Wholesome Tip

Because it has such a high sugar content, barbecue sauce often burns easily. To prevent this, brush sauce on only during the last 15 minutes of grilling or serve it on the side.

Garlic Sauce

   2 tablespoons olive oil
   1 large head of garlic, cloves separated and peeled
   2 (1-inch-wide) strips lemon peel
   1 can (14½ ounces) reduced-sodium chicken broth
   ½ cup water
   1 sprig *each* sage and oregano *or* 2 to 3 sprigs parsley
   ¼ cup butter, softened

Heat oil in a saucepan; add garlic cloves and lemon peel. Sauté over medium-low heat, stirring frequently, until garlic just starts to brown in a few spots. Add broth, water and herbs; simmer to reduce mixture by about half. Discard herb sprigs and lemon peel. Transfer broth mixture to a blender or food processor; process until smooth. Return garlic purée to the saucepan and whisk in butter over very low heat until smooth. Sauce can be rewarmed before serving.   *Makes about 1 cup*

Favorite recipe from **The Kingsford Products Company**

Wholesome Tip

This Garlic Sauce is so good you may want to double the recipe and serve it with grilled chicken.

Smucker's® Lemon Apricot Marinade

Prep Time: 5 minutes

½ cup SMUCKER'S® Apricot Preserves
¼ cup pitted green olives, sliced into quarters
   Juice and grated peel of 1 large lemon (about
     3 tablespoons juice and 1 tablespoon peel)
1 teaspoon freshly ground black pepper
¼ teaspoon salt

Combine all ingredients in a small bowl and mix well. Use marinade for grilling and basting shrimp, salmon, swordfish or chicken.

Makes 6 servings

Orange Sauce

1 tablespoon brown sugar
2 teaspoons cornstarch
 Juice of 1 orange (about ½ cup)
2 tablespoons butter
1 teaspoon grated orange peel

Combine brown sugar and cornstarch in saucepan. Add juice, butter and orange peel. Cook over medium heat, stirring constantly, until thickened. *Makes ⅔ cup*

Favorite recipe from **Wisconsin Milk Marketing Board**

Sweet 'n Zesty Barbecue Sauce

¾ **cup HOLLAND HOUSE® White Cooking Wine**
½ **cup GRANDMA'S® Molasses**
½ **cup chili sauce**
¼ **cup prepared mustard**
 1 **small onion, chopped**
 1 **tablespoon Worcestershire sauce**

In medium saucepan, combine all ingredients; mix well. Bring to a boil, reduce heat. Simmer uncovered 10 minutes.

Makes 2 cups

Wholesome Tip

This barbecue sauce will taste great on chicken, steaks or ribs.

Honey Barbecue Baste

  1 tablespoon vegetable oil
  ¼ cup minced onion
  1 clove garlic, minced
  1 can (8 ounces) tomato sauce
  ⅓ cup honey
  3 tablespoons vinegar
  2 tablespoons dry sherry
  1 teaspoon dry mustard
  ½ teaspoon salt
  ¼ teaspoon coarsely ground black pepper

Heat oil in medium saucepan over medium heat until hot. Add onion and garlic; cook and stir until onion is tender. Add remaining ingredients. Bring to a boil; reduce heat to low and simmer 20 minutes. Serve over grilled chicken, pork, spareribs, salmon or hamburgers.   *Makes 1 cup*

Favorite recipe from **National Honey Board**

Sweet 'n Spicy Onion Glaze

1 envelope LIPTON® RECIPE SECRETS® Onion Soup Mix
1 jar (20 ounces) apricot preserves
1 cup WISH-BONE® Sweet 'n Spicy French Dressing*

Also terrific with Wish-Bone® Lite Sweet 'n Spicy French-Style or Russian Dressing.

In small bowl, blend all ingredients. Remove amount of glaze you need for chicken, spareribs, kabobs, hamburgers or frankfurters. Brush on during last half of grilling, broiling or baking. Remainder of glaze can be stored covered in refrigerator up to 2 weeks.

Makes 2½ cups

Note: Recipe can be doubled.

Strawberry Daiquiri Dessert

1 package (3 ounces) ladyfingers, thawed if frozen,
    split in half horizontally
2 tablespoons light rum or apricot nectar
1 container (8 ounces) thawed frozen nondairy
    whipped topping, divided
1 package (8 ounces) cream cheese, softened
1 package (16 ounces) frozen strawberries, thawed
1 can (10 ounces) frozen strawberry daiquiri mix,
    thawed
    Fresh strawberries (optional)

Place ladyfinger halves, cut side up, in bottom of 11×7-inch dish. Brush with rum.

Reserve 1 cup whipped topping in small bowl; refrigerate, covered.

Place cream cheese in food processor; process until fluffy. Add remaining whipped topping, thawed frozen strawberries and daiquiri mix; process with on/off pulses until blended. Pour over ladyfingers.

Freeze 6 hours or overnight. Remove from freezer. Allow dish to stand at room temperature 20 to 30 minutes before serving. Garnish with remaining whipped topping and fresh strawberries, if desired. Store any leftover dessert in freezer.

Makes 10 servings

Strawberry Daiquiri Dessert

Berry Striped Pops

   2 cups strawberries
   ¾ cup honey, divided
  12 (3-ounce) paper cups or popsicle molds
  12 popsicle sticks
   6 kiwifruit, peeled and sliced
   2 cups sliced peaches

Purée strawberries with ¼ cup honey in blender or food processor. Divide mixture evenly between 12 cups or popsicle molds. Freeze about 30 minutes or until firm. Meanwhile, rinse processor; purée kiwifruit with ¼ cup honey. Repeat process with peaches and remaining ¼ cup honey. When strawberry layer is firm, pour kiwifruit purée into molds. Insert popsicle sticks and freeze about 30 minutes or until firm. Pour peach purée into molds and freeze until firm and ready to serve.

Makes 12 servings

Favorite recipe from **National Honey Board**

Tempting Apple Trifles

½ cup fat-free (skim) milk
1½ teaspoons cornstarch
4½ teaspoons dark brown sugar
1 egg white
½ teaspoon canola oil
½ teaspoon vanilla extract
½ teaspoon rum extract, divided
¼ cup unsweetened apple cider, divided
2 tablespoons raisins
½ teaspoon ground cinnamon
1 cup peeled and chopped Golden Delicious apple
1 cup ½-inch angel food cake cubes, divided

To prepare custard, combine milk and cornstarch in small, heavy saucepan; stir until cornstarch is completely dissolved. Add brown sugar, egg white and oil; blend well. Slowly bring to a boil over medium-low heat until thickened, stirring constantly with whisk. Remove from heat; stir in vanilla and ¼ teaspoon rum extract. Set aside; cool completely.

Combine 2 tablespoons cider, raisins and cinnamon in medium saucepan; bring to a boil over medium-low heat. Add apple and cook until apple is fork-tender and all liquid has been absorbed, stirring frequently. Remove from heat; set aside to cool.

To assemble, place ¼ cup cake cubes in bottom of 2 small trifle or dessert dishes. Combine remaining 2 tablespoons cider and ¼ teaspoon rum extract in small bowl; mix well. Spoon 1½ teaspoons cider mixture over cake in each dish. Top each with ¼ of custard mixture and ¼ cup cooked apple mixture. Repeat layers. Serve immediately. Garnish with fresh mint, if desired.

Makes 2 servings

Buttery Lemon Bars

Crust
   1¼ **cups all-purpose flour**
   ½ **cup butter, softened**
   ¼ **cup powdered sugar**
   ½ **teaspoon vanilla**

Filling
   1 **cup granulated sugar**
   2 **eggs**
   ⅓ **cup fresh lemon juice**
   2 **tablespoons all-purpose flour**
   Grated peel of 1 lemon
   Powdered sugar

1. Preheat oven to 350°F.

2. Combine all crust ingredients in small bowl. Beat 2 to 3 minutes until mixture is crumbly. Press onto bottom of 8-inch square baking pan. Bake 15 to 20 minutes or until edges are lightly browned.

3. Combine all filling ingredients except powdered sugar in small bowl. Beat until well mixed.

4. Pour filling over hot crust. Continue baking 15 to 18 minutes or until filling is set. Sprinkle with powdered sugar; cool completely. Cut into bars; sprinkle again with powdered sugar.

Makes about 16 bars

Spiced Grilled Bananas

3 large ripe firm bananas
¼ cup golden raisins
3 tablespoons packed brown sugar
½ teaspoon ground cinnamon
¼ teaspoon ground nutmeg
¼ teaspoon ground cardamom or coriander
2 tablespoons margarine, cut into 8 pieces
1 tablespoon fresh lime juice
Vanilla low-fat frozen yogurt (optional)
Additional fresh lime juice (optional)

1. Spray grillproof 9-inch pie plate with nonstick cooking spray. Cut bananas diagonally into ½-inch-thick slices. Arrange, overlapping, in prepared pie plate. Sprinkle with raisins.

2. Combine sugar, cinnamon, nutmeg and cardamom in small bowl; sprinkle over bananas and raisins and dot with margarine pieces. Cover pie plate tightly with foil. Place on grid and grill, covered, over low coals 10 to 15 minutes or until bananas are hot and tender.

3. Carefully remove foil and sprinkle with 1 tablespoon lime juice. Serve over low-fat frozen yogurt and sprinkle with additional lime juice, if desired. Garnish as desired.   *Makes 4 servings*

Mini Cherry Cheesecakes

Prep Time: 15 minutes
Freeze Time: 3 hours

    12 NILLA® Wafers
    1 package (8 ounces) PHILADELPHIA® Cream Cheese,
      softened
    ¾ cup sugar
    1 tub (8 ounces) COOL WHIP® Whipped Topping,
      thawed
    1 cup cherry pie filling

PLACE 1 wafer into bottom of each of 12 (2½-inch) paper-lined muffin cups; set aside.

BEAT cream cheese and sugar with electric mixer on medium speed or wire whisk until light and fluffy. Stir in ½ of the whipped topping. Spoon filling into each cup, filling about ⅔ full. Top with cherry pie filling.

FREEZE 3 hours or until firm. To serve, let stand at room temperature 15 minutes. Serve with additional whipped topping, if desired. *Makes 12 servings*

Helpful Hint: Soften cream cheese in microwave on HIGH 15 to 20 seconds.

Great Substitute: Strawberry, raspberry or lemon pie filling can be substituted for the cherry pie filling.

Mango Vanilla Parfait

½ (4-serving size) package vanilla sugar-free instant
   pudding mix
1¼ cups fat-free (skim) milk
½ cup mango cubes
2 large strawberries, sliced
3 sugar-free shortbread cookies, crumbled *or*
   2 tablespoons reduced-fat granola
Strawberry slices for garnish

1. Prepare pudding according to package directions using 1¼ cups milk.

2. In parfait glass or small glass bowl, layer quarter of pudding, half of mango, half of strawberries and quarter of pudding. Repeat layers in second parfait glass. Refrigerate 30 minutes.

3. Just before serving, top with cookie crumbs and garnish with strawberries.   *Makes 2 servings*

Chocolate Chip Ice Cream Sandwiches

1¼ cups firmly packed light brown sugar
¾ Butter Flavor CRISCO® Stick or ¾ cup Butter Flavor
    CRISCO® all-vegetable shortening
  2 tablespoons milk
  1 tablespoon vanilla
  1 egg
1¾ cups all-purpose flour
  1 teaspoon salt
¾ teaspoon baking soda
  1 cup semisweet chocolate chips
  1 cup chopped pecans
  2 pints ice cream, any flavor

1. Heat oven to 375°F. Place sheets of foil on countertop for cooling cookies.

2. Place brown sugar, shortening, milk and vanilla in large bowl. Beat at medium speed of electric mixer until well blended. Add egg; beat well.

3. Combine flour, salt and baking soda. Add to shortening mixture; beat at low speed just until blended. Stir in chocolate chips and pecans.

4. Measure ¼ cup dough; shape into ball. Repeat with remaining dough. Place balls 4 inches apart on ungreased baking sheets. Flatten balls into 3-inch circles.

5. Bake one baking sheet at a time at 375°F for 10 to 12 minutes or until cookies are lightly browned. *Do not overbake.* Cool 2 minutes on baking sheet. Remove cookies to foil to cool completely.

continued on page 195

Delightful Desserts - 194

Chocolate Chip Ice Cream Sandwiches, continued

6. Remove ice cream from freezer to soften slightly. Measure ½ cup ice cream; spread onto bottom of one cookie. Cover with flat side of second cookie. Wrap sandwich in plastic wrap. Place in freezer. Repeat with remaining cookies and ice cream.

Makes about 10 ice cream sandwiches

Note: Chocolate Chip Ice Cream Sandwiches should be eaten within two days. After two days, cookies will absorb moisture and become soggy. If longer storage is needed, make and freeze cookies, but assemble ice cream sandwiches within two days of serving.

The Wild Berry Sundae

Blueberries, raspberries, blackberries and/or
  strawberries, rinsed and patted dry
Scoops of vanilla ice cream
HERSHEY'S Chocolate Shoppe™ Hot Fudge Topping
REDDI-WIP® Whipped Topping

• Alternate layers of berries with ice cream and HERSHEY'S Chocolate Shoppe Hot Fudge topping in sundae dish.

• Top with REDDI-WIP Whipped Topping.   *Makes 1 sundae*

Delightful Desserts - 195

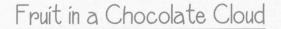

Fruit in a Chocolate Cloud

   Yogurt Cheese (recipe follows)
   2 cups (1 pint) fresh strawberries, rinsed and drained
   ¼ cup sugar
   **¼ cup HERSHEY¡S Cocoa or HERSHEY¡S Dutch
      Processed Cocoa**
   2 tablespoons hot water
   2 teaspoons vanilla extract, divided
   ½ to 1 teaspoon freshly grated orange peel (optional)
   2 envelopes (1.3 ounces *each*) dry whipped topping mix
   1 cup cold nonfat milk
   2 large bananas, sliced

1. Prepare Yogurt Cheese a day in advance.

2. Remove hulls of strawberries; cut strawberries in half vertically.

3. Stir together sugar, cocoa and water in medium bowl until
smooth and well blended. Stir in 1 teaspoon vanilla. Gradually stir
in Yogurt Cheese and orange peel, if desired; blend thoroughly.

4. Prepare topping mixes in large bowl as directed on packages,
using 1 cup milk and remaining 1 teaspoon vanilla; fold into
chocolate mixture. Carefully spoon half of chocolate mixture into
1½-quart glass serving bowl; place one-half of strawberry halves,
cut sides out, around inside of entire bowl. Layer banana slices
over chocolate mixture. Cut remaining strawberry halves into
smaller pieces; layer over banana slices. Carefully spread
remaining chocolate mixture over fruit. Cover; refrigerate several
hours before serving. Garnish as desired.   *Makes 12 servings*

Yogurt Cheese: Use two 8-ounce containers vanilla lowfat yogurt,
no gelatin added. Line non-rusting colander or sieve with large
piece of double thickness cheesecloth or large coffee filter; place
colander over deep bowl. Spoon yogurt into prepared colander;
cover with plastic wrap. Refrigerate until liquid no longer drains
from yogurt, about 24 hours. Remove yogurt from cheesecloth
and place in separate bowl; discard liquid.

Cheery Cherry Brownies

¾ **cup all-purpose flour**
½ **cup no-calorie sweetener**
½ **cup unsweetened cocoa powder**
¼ **teaspoon baking soda**
½ **cup evaporated fat-free milk**
⅓ **cup butter, melted**
¼ **cup cholesterol-free egg substitute**
¼ **cup honey**
 1 **teaspoon vanilla**
½ **(15½-ounce) can pitted tart red cherries, drained and
    halved**

1. Preheat oven to 350°F. Grease 11×7-inch baking pan; set aside.

2. Stir together flour, sweetener, cocoa powder and baking soda in large mixing bowl. Add milk, butter, egg substitute, honey and vanilla. Stir just until mixed.

3. Pour into prepared pan. Sprinkle cherries over top of chocolate mixture. Bake 13 to 15 minutes or until wooden pick inserted into center comes out clean. Cool. Cut into 12 equal-size brownies.

Makes 12 servings

Nectarine Blueberry Crisp

3 cups cubed unpeeled nectarines
2 cups fresh blueberries
2 tablespoons granulated sugar
1 tablespoon cornstarch
½ teaspoon ground cinnamon
¼ cup all-purpose flour
¼ cup uncooked quick oats
¼ cup chopped walnuts
3 tablespoons dark brown sugar
2 tablespoons toasted wheat germ
2 tablespoons reduced-fat margarine, melted
¼ teaspoon ground nutmeg

1. Preheat oven to 400°F. Spray bottom and side of 9-inch round or square baking pan with nonstick cooking spray. Combine nectarines, blueberries, granulated sugar, cornstarch and cinnamon in medium bowl. Transfer to prepared pan; bake 15 minutes.

2. Meanwhile, combine remaining ingredients in small bowl, stirring with fork until crumbly. Remove fruit mixture from oven; sprinkle with topping. Return to oven; bake 20 minutes longer or until fruit is bubbly and topping is lightly browned. Serve warm.

Makes 6 servings

Creamy Cappuccino Frozen Dessert

Make-Ahead Time: 1 day or up to 1 week before serving
Final Prep/Stand Time: 15 minutes

1 package (8 ounces) cream cheese, softened
1 can (14 ounces) sweetened condensed milk
½ cup chocolate syrup
1 tablespoon instant coffee powder
1 tablespoon hot water
1½ cups thawed frozen whipped topping
1 prepared chocolate crumb crust (6 ounces)
¼ cup chopped pecans, toasted
Additional chocolate syrup

1. Beat cream cheese in large mixing bowl on medium speed of electric mixer for 2 to 3 minutes or until fluffy. Add sweetened condensed milk and ½ cup syrup; beat on low speed until well blended.

2. Dissolve coffee powder in hot water in small bowl. Slowly stir into cream cheese mixture. Fold in whipped topping; spoon mixture into crust. Sprinkle with pecans. Cover and freeze overnight.

3. Let dessert stand in refrigerator 10 to 15 minutes before serving. Cut into wedges. Drizzle with additional syrup.

Makes 16 servings

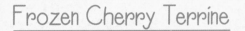

Frozen Cherry Terrine

1 can (8 ounces) pitted dark sweet cherries in light
   syrup, undrained
1 cup boiling water
1 package (4-serving size) JELL-O® Brand Cherry Flavor
   Sugar Free Low-Calorie Gelatin
1 container (8 ounces) plain lowfat yogurt
2 cups thawed COOL WHIP LITE® Whipped Topping

• Line bottom and sides of 9×5-inch loaf pan with plastic wrap;
set aside.

• Drain cherries, reserving syrup. If necessary, add enough cold
water to reserved syrup to measure ½ cup. Cut cherries into
quarters.

• Stir boiling water into gelatin in large bowl at least 2 minutes
until completely dissolved. Add measured syrup. Stir in yogurt
until well blended. Chill until mixture is thickened but not set,
about 45 minutes to 1 hour, stirring occasionally. Gently stir in
cherries and whipped topping. Pour into prepared pan; cover.
Freeze until firm, about 6 hours or overnight.

• Remove pan from freezer about 15 minutes before serving. Let
stand at room temperature to soften slightly. Remove plastic
wrap. Cut into slices.   *Makes 12 servings*

Note: Cover and store leftover terrine in freezer.

Chocolate-Caramel S'Mores

12 chocolate wafer cookies or chocolate graham cracker squares
2 tablespoons fat-free caramel topping
6 large marshmallows

1. Prepare coals for grilling. Place 6 wafer cookies top-down on a plate. Spread 1 teaspoon caramel topping in center of each wafer to within about ¼-inch of edge.

2. Spear 1 to 2 marshmallows onto long wood-handled skewers.* Hold several inches above coals 3 to 5 minutes until marshmallows are golden and very soft, turning slowly. Push 1 marshmallow off into center of caramel. Top with plain wafer. Repeat with remaining marshmallows and wafers.   *Makes 6 servings*

If wood-handled skewers are unavailable, use oven mitt to protect hand from heat.

Wholesome Tip

S'mores, a favorite campfire treat, got their name because everyone who tasted them wanted "some more." In the unlikely event of leftover S'mores, they can be reheated in the microwave at HIGH 15 to 30 seconds.

Fruit Pizza

1 (20-ounce) package refrigerated sugar cookie dough
1 (8-ounce) package cream cheese, softened
1 cup powdered sugar
   Assorted fresh fruit (strawberries, bananas, kiwifruit,
      blueberries, mandarin oranges, etc.)
½ cup SMUCKER'S® Apricot Preserves or Sweet Orange
   Marmalade
1 tablespoon water

Cut dough into 1-inch slices and place on ungreased cookie sheet or pizza pan. Bake 17 to 19 minutes or until light golden brown around edges. Cool.

Combine cream cheese and sugar; mix well. Spread over cookies. Decorate with sliced fruit. (Dip banana slices in lemon juice to prevent browning.) Combine preserves and water; mix well. Drizzle over fruit topping. Serve immediately or refrigerate until serving time.   *Makes 9 servings*

Cherry-Peach Pops

⅓ cup peach nectar or apricot nectar
1 teaspoon unflavored gelatin
1 (15-ounce) can sliced peaches in light syrup, drained
1 (6- or 8-ounce) carton fat-free peach yogurt with
    sweetener
1 (6- or 8-ounce) carton fat-free cherry yogurt with
    sweetener

1. Combine nectar and unflavored gelatin in small saucepan; let stand 5 minutes. Heat and stir over low heat just until gelatin dissolves.

2. Combine nectar mixture, drained peaches and yogurts. Cover and blend until smooth.

3. Pour into 7 (3-ounce) paper cups, filling each about ⅔ full. Place in freezer; freeze 1 hour. Insert wooden stick into center of each cup. Freeze at least 3 more hours.

4. Let stand at room temperature 10 minutes before serving. Tear away paper cups to serve. *Makes 7 servings*

Citrus Sorbet

Prep Time: 20 minutes
Freeze Time: 20 minutes

**1 can (12 ounces) DOLE® Orange Peach Mango or
  Tropical Fruit Frozen Juice Concentrate
1 can (8 ounces) DOLE® Crushed Pineapple or Pineapple
  Tidbits, drained
½ cup plain nonfat or low fat yogurt
2½ cups cold water**

• Combine frozen juice concentrate, crushed pineapple and
yogurt in blender or food processor container; blend until smooth.
Stir in water.

• Pour mixture into container of ice cream maker.* Freeze
according to manufacturer's directions.

• Serve sorbet in dessert dishes.   *Makes 10 servings*

*Or, pour sorbet mixture into 8-inch square metal pan; cover. Freeze
1½ to 2 hours or until slightly firm. Place in large bowl; beat with electric
mixer on medium speed 1 minute or until slushy. Return mixture to metal
pan; repeat freezing and beating steps. Freeze until firm, about 6 hours
or overnight.*

Passion-Banana Sorbet: Substitute DOLE® Pine-Orange-Banana
Frozen Juice Concentrate for frozen juice concentrate. Prepare
sorbet as directed above except reduce water to 2 cups and omit
canned pineapple.

Peach Blueberry Cheesecake

Crust
- 1½ cups crushed graham cracker crumbs
- ½ cup crushed gingersnap cookies
- 5 tablespoons butter, melted

Filling
- 2 packages (8 ounces each) cream cheese, softened
- ¾ cup sugar
- ½ cup GRANDMA'S® Molasses
- 7 egg yolks
- 2 tablespoons lemon juice
- 1½ teaspoons vanilla extract
- ½ teaspoon salt
- 3 cups sour cream

Topping
- 1 can (16 ounces) peach slices, drained
- Fresh blueberries
- 2 tablespoons peach or apricot preserves, melted

1. Heat oven to 350°F. Grease 9-inch springform pan. In small bowl, combine crust ingredients; press over bottom and half way up side of pan. Refrigerate. Place large roasting pan filled with 1 inch hot water on middle rack of oven. In large bowl, beat cream cheese and sugar until very smooth, about 3 minutes. Beat in molasses. Add egg yolks, beating until batter is smooth. Add lemon juice, vanilla and salt; beat until well incorporated. Beat in sour cream just until blended. Pour batter into prepared crust.

2. Place cheesecake in large roasting pan. Bake 45 minutes. Turn oven off without opening door and let cake cool 1 hour. Transfer cheesecake to wire rack (center will be jiggly) and cool to room temperature, about 1 hour. Cover pan with plastic wrap and refrigerate overnight. Remove side of pan. Top with peach slices and blueberries. Brush fruit with preserves.

Makes 12 to 16 servings

Fruitful Frozen Yogurt

1 envelope unflavored gelatin
¼ cup cold water
1½ cups puréed fresh fruit
1 carton (16 ounces) vanilla low-fat yogurt
¼ to ½ cup sugar

1. Sprinkle gelatin over cold water in small saucepan; let stand 5 minutes to soften. Stir over low heat until gelatin dissolves. Remove from heat. Stir in fruit purée, yogurt and sugar to taste. Pour into 9-inch square pan; freeze until almost firm.

2. Coarsely chop mixture; spoon into chilled bowl. Beat with electric mixer until smooth. Cover; store in freezer.

Makes 5 servings

Tip: Use dark fruits like strawberries, raspberries or cherries to make this recipe as pleasing to the eye as it is to the palate.

Favorite recipe from **Wisconsin Milk Marketing Board**

White & Chocolate
Covered Strawberries

1⅔ cups (10-ounce package) HERSHEY'S Premier White Chips
2 tablespoons shortening (do not use butter, margarine, spread or oil)
1 cup HERSHEY'S Semi-Sweet Chocolate Chips
4 cups (2 pints) fresh strawberries, rinsed, patted dry and chilled

1. Cover tray with wax paper.

2. Place white chips and 1 tablespoon shortening in medium microwave-safe bowl. Microwave at HIGH (100%) 1 minute; stir until chips are melted and mixture is smooth. If necessary, microwave at HIGH an additional 30 seconds at a time, just until smooth when stirred.

3. Holding by top, dip ⅔ of each strawberry into white chip mixture; shake gently to remove excess. Place on prepared tray; refrigerate until coating is firm, at least 30 minutes.

4. Repeat microwave procedure with chocolate chips in clean microwave-safe bowl. Dip lower ⅓ of each berry into chocolate mixture. Refrigerate until firm. Cover; refrigerate leftover strawberries.   *Makes 2 to 3 dozen berries*

Triple Chocolate Cheesecakes

Prep Time: 20 minutes
Chill Time: 4 hours

- **1 envelope unflavored gelatin**
- **½ cup cold water**
- **2 (8-ounce) packages cream cheese, softened**
- **1 (14-ounce) can EAGLE® BRAND Sweetened Condensed Milk (NOT evaporated milk)**
- **4 (1-ounce) squares unsweetened chocolate, melted and slightly cooled**
- **1 (8-ounce) carton frozen non-dairy whipped topping, thawed**
- **½ cup (3 ounces) mini semi-sweet chocolate chips**
- **1 (21-ounce) can cherry pie filling, if desired**
- **2 (6-ounce) ready-made chocolate crumb pie crusts**

1. In 1-cup glass measure, combine gelatin and cold water; let stand 5 minutes to soften. Pour about 1 inch water into small saucepan; place glass measure in saucepan. Place saucepan over medium heat; stir until gelatin is dissolved. Remove measure from saucepan; cool slightly.

2. In large mixing bowl, combine cream cheese, Eagle Brand and melted chocolate; beat until smooth. Gradually beat in gelatin mixture. Fold in whipped topping and chips.

3. Spread pie filling on bottoms of crusts, if desired. Spoon chocolate mixture into pie crusts. Cover and chill at least 4 hours. Store covered in refrigerator.

Makes 2 cheesecakes (12 servings total)

Tip: To store these cheesecakes in the freezer, cover and freeze them for up to 1 month. Serve the cheesecakes frozen, or remove them from the freezer several hours before serving and let them thaw in the refrigerator.

Watermelon Ice

4 cups seeded 1-inch watermelon chunks
¼ cup thawed frozen unsweetened pineapple juice
concentrate
2 tablespoons fresh lime juice
Fresh melon balls (optional)
Fresh mint leaves (optional)

Place melon chunks in single layer in plastic freezer bag; freeze until firm, about 8 hours. Place frozen melon in food processor container fitted with steel blade. Let stand 15 minutes to soften slightly. Add pineapple juice and lime juice. Remove plunger from top of food processor to allow air to be incorporated. Process until smooth, scraping down sides of container frequently. Spoon into individual dessert dishes. Garnish with melon balls and mint leaves, if desired. Freeze leftovers. *Makes 6 servings*

Honeydew Ice: Substitute honeydew for watermelon and unsweetened pineapple-guava-orange juice concentrate for pineapple juice concentrate.

Cantaloupe Ice: Substitute cantaloupe for watermelon and unsweetened pineapple-guava-orange juice concentrate for pineapple juice concentrate.

Note: Ices may be transferred to airtight container and frozen up to 1 month. Let stand at room temperature 10 minutes to soften slightly before serving.

Oatmeal Coconut Chocolate Chip Cookies

Cookies
> 1 Butter Flavor CRISCO® Stick or 1 cup Butter Flavor
> CRISCO® all-vegetable shortening plus additional for
> greasing
> 1 cup granulated sugar
> ½ cup firmly packed light brown sugar
> 2 eggs
> 2 teaspoons vanilla
> 2 cups all-purpose flour
> 1 teaspoon salt
> 1 teaspoon baking soda
> ⅔ cup quick oats, uncooked
> ½ cup flake coconut
> 1 cup semi-sweet chocolate chips

Chocolate Coating
> 1 cup semi-sweet chocolate chips
> 2 teaspoons Butter Flavor CRISCO® Stick or 2 teaspoons
> Butter Flavor CRISCO® all-vegetable shortening

1. Heat oven to 375°F. Grease baking sheet with shortening. Place sheets of foil on countertop for cooling cookies.

2. For cookies, combine 1 cup shortening, granulated sugar, brown sugar, eggs and vanilla in large bowl. Beat at medium speed of electric mixer until well blended.

3. Combine flour, salt and baking soda. Add gradually to creamed mixture at low speed. Beat until well blended. Stir in oats, coconut and 1 cup chocolate chips with spoon. Drop by teaspoonfuls 2 inches apart onto prepared baking sheet.

4. Bake at 375°F for 10 to 12 minutes or until light brown. *Do not overbake.* Cool 2 minutes on baking sheet. Remove cookies to foil to cool completely.

continued on page 211

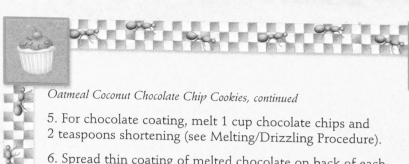

5. For chocolate coating, melt 1 cup chocolate chips and 2 teaspoons shortening (see Melting/Drizzling Procedure).

6. Spread thin coating of melted chocolate on back of each cookie. Place upside down on waxed paper to allow coating to harden.   *Makes about 6 dozen cookies*

Melting/Drizzling Procedure: For melting or drizzling, choose one of these easy methods. Start with chips and Butter Flavor Crisco® all-vegetable shortening (if called for), then: place in small microwave-safe measuring cup or bowl. Microwave at 50% (MEDIUM). Stir after 1 minute. Repeat until smooth. Drizzle from tip of spoon. Or, place chips and shortening in heavy resealable plastic sandwich bag. Seal. Microwave at 50% (MEDIUM). Check every minute until melted. Knead bag until smooth. Cut tiny tip off corner of bag. Squeeze out to drizzle. Or, place chips and shortening in small saucepan. Melt on range top on very low heat. Stir until smooth. Drizzle from tip of spoon.

Easy Citrus Berry Shortcake

1 individual sponge cake
1 tablespoon orange juice
¼ cup lemon chiffon sugar-free, nonfat yogurt
¼ cup thawed frozen fat-free nondairy whipped topping
⅔ cup sliced strawberries or raspberries
Mint leaves (optional)

1. Place sponge cake on serving plate. Drizzle with orange juice.

2. Fold together yogurt and whipped topping. Spoon half of mixture onto cake. Top with berries and remaining yogurt mixture. Garnish with mint leaves, if desired.

Makes 1 serving

Barbecue Banana Split

1 banana
Butter, melted
Brown sugar
Ice cream
Chocolate sauce
Whipped cream, nuts, maraschino cherry

Cut firm, ripe banana lengthwise to, but not through, bottom peel. Brush cut sides with melted butter; sprinkle with a little brown sugar. Grill 6 to 8 minutes on covered grill over medium-hot KINGSFORD® Briquets until banana is heated through but still firm (peel will turn dark). Place unpeeled banana in serving dish; top with small scoops of ice cream. Drizzle with chocolate or caramel sauce. Top with whipped cream, nuts and a cherry.

Makes 1 serving

Wholesome Tip

Be creative with your sundae toppings. Choose your favorite chopped candy bars, crushed cookies and sprinkles.

Peach Ice Cream

7 fresh California peaches, peeled, halved and pitted
2 cups 2% low-fat milk
1 envelope unflavored gelatin
1 cup plain low-fat yogurt
½ cup sugar
1 tablespoon vanilla

Chop enough peaches to measure 1 cup. Add remaining peaches to food processor or blender; process to measure 2½ cups purée. Combine milk and gelatin in medium saucepan. Heat, stirring, until gelatin dissolves; remove from heat. Add chopped peaches, peach purée, yogurt, sugar and vanilla to gelatin mixture; mix well. Prepare in ice cream maker according to manufacturer's directions. Transfer to freezing containers and freeze until firm.

Makes 7 servings

Favorite recipe from **California Tree Fruit Agreement**

Delightful Desserts - 213

Chocolate-Covered Banana Pops

3 ripe large bananas
9 wooden popsicle sticks
2 cups (12-ounce package) HERSHEY'S Semi-Sweet
   Chocolate Chips
2 tablespoons shortening (do *not* use butter, margarine,
   spread or oil)
1½ cups coarsely chopped unsalted, roasted peanuts

1. Peel bananas; cut each into thirds. Insert a wooden stick into each banana piece; place on wax paper-covered tray. Cover; freeze until firm.

2. Place chocolate chips and shortening in medium microwave-safe bowl. Microwave at HIGH (100%) 1½ to 2 minutes or until chocolate is melted and mixture is smooth when stirred.

3. Remove bananas from freezer just before dipping. Dip each piece into warm chocolate, covering completely; allow excess to drip off. Immediately roll in peanuts. Cover; return to freezer. Serve frozen. *Makes 9 pops*

Variation: HERSHEY'S Milk Chocolate Chips or HERSHEY'S MINI CHIPS® Semi-Sweet Chocolate Chips may be substituted for Semi-Sweet Chocolate Chips.

Neopolitan Chip Bomb

Prep Time: 25 minutes plus freezing

30 CHIPS AHOY!® Chocolate Chip Cookies, divided
½ gallon vanilla, chocolate and strawberry ice cream,
 softened
 1 tub (8 ounces) COOL WHIP® Whipped Topping,
 thawed

CUT 6 cookies in half. Reserve 1 whole cookie and cookie halves for garnish.

LINE 2½ quart bowl with plastic wrap. Separate 3 flavors of ice cream. Press 1 flavor into bowl. Arrange layer of cookies over ice cream. Repeat procedure to make 2 more layers, ending with cookies. Cover with plastic wrap.

FREEZE 4 hours or overnight. Invert bomb onto large serving plate. Remove plastic wrap. Frost with whipped topping. Garnish with reserved cookies. Let stand at room temperature about 10 minutes for easier cutting and serving.   *Makes 12 servings*

Great Substitute: Try other flavors of ice cream.

The publisher would like to thank
the companies and organizations listed below for the use
of their recipes and photographs in this publication.

A.1.® Steak Sauce
Barilla America, Inc.
Birds Eye®
Butterball® Turkey Company
California Tree Fruit Agreement
ConAgra Foods®
Del Monte Corporation
Dole Food Company, Inc.
Eagle® Brand
Filippo Berio® Olive Oil
The Fremont Company, Makers of Frank's &
SnowFloss Kraut and Tomato Products
Grandma's® is a registered trademark of Mott's, Inc.
Grey Poupon® Dijon Mustard
Heinz U.S.A.
Hershey Foods Corporation
The Hidden Valley® Food Products Company
Holland House® is a registered trademark of Mott's, Inc.
The Kingsford Products Company
Kraft Foods Holdings
Lawry's® Foods, Inc.
Mauna La'i® is a registered trademark of Mott's, Inc.
McIlhenny Company (TABASCO® brand Pepper Sauce)
Mushroom Council
National Chicken Council / US Poultry & Egg Association
National Fisheries Institute
National Honey Board
National Pork Board
National Turkey Federation
North Dakota Beef Commission
Perdue Farms Incorporated
Plochman, Inc.
Reckitt Benckiser Inc.
Reddi-wip® is a registered trademark of ConAgra Brands, Inc.
Riviana Foods Inc.
Sargento® Foods Inc.
The J.M. Smucker Company
StarKist® Seafood Company
Uncle Ben's Inc.
Unilever Bestfoods North America
Wisconsin Milk Marketing Board

METRIC CONVERSION CHART

VOLUME MEASUREMENTS (dry)

1/8 teaspoon = 0.5 mL
1/4 teaspoon = 1 mL
1/2 teaspoon = 2 mL
3/4 teaspoon = 4 mL
1 teaspoon = 5 mL
1 tablespoon = 15 mL
2 tablespoons = 30 mL
1/4 cup = 60 mL
1/3 cup = 75 mL
1/2 cup = 125 mL
2/3 cup = 150 mL
3/4 cup = 175 mL
1 cup = 250 mL
2 cups = 1 pint = 500 mL
3 cups = 750 mL
4 cups = 1 quart = 1 L

VOLUME MEASUREMENTS (fluid)

1 fluid ounce (2 tablespoons) = 30 mL
4 fluid ounces (1/2 cup) = 125 mL
8 fluid ounces (1 cup) = 250 mL
12 fluid ounces (1 1/2 cups) = 375 mL
16 fluid ounces (2 cups) = 500 mL

WEIGHTS (mass)

1/2 ounce = 15 g
1 ounce = 30 g
3 ounces = 90 g
4 ounces = 120 g
8 ounces = 225 g
10 ounces = 285 g
12 ounces = 360 g
16 ounces = 1 pound = 450 g

DIMENSIONS

1/16 inch = 2 mm
1/8 inch = 3 mm
1/4 inch = 6 mm
1/2 inch = 1.5 cm
3/4 inch = 2 cm
1 inch = 2.5 cm

OVEN TEMPERATURES

250°F = 120°C
275°F = 140°C
300°F = 150°C
325°F = 160°C
350°F = 180°C
375°F = 190°C
400°F = 200°C
425°F = 220°C
450°F = 230°C

BAKING PAN SIZES

Utensil	Size in Inches/Quarts	Metric Volume	Size in Centimeters
Baking or	8×8×2	2 L	20×20×5
Cake Pan	9×9×2	2.5 L	23×23×5
(square or	12×8×2	3 L	30×20×5
rectangular)	13×9×2	3.5 L	33×23×5
Loaf Pan	8×4×3	1.5 L	20×10×7
	9×5×3	2 L	23×13×7
Round Layer	8×1½	1.2 L	20×4
Cake Pan	9×1½	1.5 L	23×4
Pie Plate	8×1¼	750 mL	20×3
	9×1¼	1 L	23×3
Baking Dish	1 quart	1 L	—
or Casserole	1½ quart	1.5 L	—
	2 quart	2 L	—